For Terry
& John
my favorite
Texans!
from

Barnaby

Books by Barnaby Conrad

Fiction

The Innocent Villa
Matador
Dangerfield
Zorro: A Fox in the City
Endangered (with Niels Mortensen)
Fire Below Zero (with Nico Mastorakis)
Keepers of the Secret (with Nico Mastorakis)

Translations

The Wounds of Hunger (Spota)
The Second Life of Captain Contreras (Luca de Tena)
My Life as a Matador (Autobiography of Carlos Arruza)

Nonfiction

Name Dropping
The Complete Guide to Writing Fiction
Hemingway's Spain
Time Is All We Have
A Revolting Transaction
Fun While It Lasted
How to Fight a Bull
Encyclopedia of Bullfighting
Tahiti
Famous Last Words
San Francisco—Profile in Words and Pictures
Death of Manolete
Gates of Fear
La Fiesta Brava

Name Dropping

Tales from My San Francisco Nightclub

Barnaby Conrad

Wild Coconuts Publishing Company

Name Dropping: Tales from My San Francisco Nightclub. Copyright ©1997 by Barnaby Conrad. All rights reserved. Printed in the United States of America. No part of this book may be used or reproduced in any manner whatsoever without written permission except in the case of brief quotations embodied in critical articles and reviews. For information address Wild Coconuts Publishing Company, 75 Water Street, San Francisco, CA 94133

Cover design by Carrie Leeb, Leeb & Sons, San Francisco

Distributed by ACCESS Publishers Network, Grawn, Michigan

First Paperback Edition

Library of Congress Catalog Card Number: 96-61771

ISBN 0-9649701-4-7

This edition is printed on acid-free paper that meets the American National Standards Institute Z39.48 Standard

Contents

For my son, Winston—
whose idea it was.

When San Francisco hills are leveled, when the flower stands are gone, when there's no more red wine and garlic on Telegraph Hill, no more hungry artists on Montgomery Street, no more Chinese children laughing in Portsmouth Square, and no more cable cars rattling up Powell Street and California Street and Jones Street and Hyde, then San Francisco will take its place as a good, realistic, modern city of industry, and the color and the romance will be gone. There'll be nothing left but memories, and as new generations are born, even the memories will disappear.

Samuel Dickson, 1957, TALES OF SAN FRANCISCO

Foreword

THE FIFTIES: We were still drinking and smoking and driving cars that began to sprout tailfins. Our fine ladies wore fur coats and long fingernails and gathered under flowery hats to lunch and gossip at El Prado. The first highrise went up on Montgomery, the shape of things to come. The town had great jazz joints—Blackhawk, Jazz Workshop, Jack's, Jimbo's— and wonderful bars, especially the Matador. We dieted by eating only steaks and baked potatoes at Grison's. When we went on the wagon, we drank Calso. The beatniks were born. The term, wrote Norman Mailer, was coined by "an idiot columnist in San Francisco."

Name dropping has a bad name. Pushy, say some. Last resort of the socially insecure. Reflected glory. A pathetic attempt to appear important through the accident of propinquity. A cheap way to become the cynosure of all ears at boring dinner parties.

All or none of the foregoing may be true. I take no sides on the issue, one that is tearing at the very fabric of society and the roots of the Republic. To drop or not to drop—it depends on the game and the player. I tend to look kindly on name dropping by people I like. Few things are more repellent than moniker-mongering by a brown-nosing arriviste, especially when the name being dropped belongs to a person you have long admired and who appears to be quite fond of the obnoxious bugger telling the tale.

There are a few rules, unofficial but universal. The name being dropped must be of the household variety, at least. If the reaction is "Who?" the game is lost. If the dropper then makes the fatal mistake of trying to identify the droppee—to no avail—there is no way out except via the back door. Another rule: The name must be accompanied by an anecdote, amusing, shocking, or both. Third, the anecdote should be apropos to the general conversation that had been flourishing till the dropper stopped it cold with his, "Say, that reminds me . . . "

For example, say the conversation is about overly critical music critics, a popular topic among people without much to talk about. The host says, "The opera was wonderful. The audience was on its feet cheering, and our stupid critic says it was the worst performance he ever heard." As everyone nods "I loved it, too" and "What do critics know anyway?" you are permitted to say in a soft but authoritative tone, "Well, as Artur Schnabel once remarked to me, 'Audiences always applaud, even when it's good.'" Silence. You have scored a point and lost a dozen friends. "Who's Artur Schnabel?" is the only possible response.

The great practitioners of name dropping—those who are invited back—are those who know what to drop and when to hold back. Their timing must be impeccable. They have to possess an encyclopedic memory and the gift of instant recall. Further, their interest in people of great prominence should be innocent, abiding, and all-consuming. They have to believe that important people really are. The game is not worth the candle if you come to the cynical conclusion that celebrities are just like anybody else, because, in truth, they aren't. The one thing celebrities have in common is that they all know each other, but not you.

Barnaby Conrad, the author of this book, is the best name dropper I know, mainly because he has never lost his innocence. He truly admires accomplished people, and he is such an engaging and amusing chap himself that they soon come to admire him. This makes him a world champion, a winner of the gold in this game with so many losers. While the rest of us lag shyly in the background, Barnaby makes it his business and pleasure to chat up the celebrity at hand, and they soon go off into the night, arm in arm, to begin a lifelong friendship. This makes the rest of us feel even more insecure.

For many years, Barnaby was in the perfect position to meet the great and the near-great. Nightly, he was master of the revels in a San Francisco boîte called El Matador, named for his best-selling novel of the same name. See, I am name dropping here. "One of my oldest friends is Barnaby Conrad." "Who?" "You know, the man who wrote *Matador?*" "Oh!" In Casablanca, it was said, "Everybody goes to Rick's." In San Francisco, for a gaudy decade when the world was young, everybody who was anybody came to El Matador, and among the anybodies was a bonanza of Somebodies.

They all loved Barnaby because he loved them with a flame that burned clean, true, and unwavering. He basked in their glow and they glowed in his pleasure at their presence. It was a great time to be making the rounds in a San Francisco that would never again be elite and small and special. The Matador has vanished, and most of the famous people who frequented the place— and had the times of their lives—have disappeared from a world grown old. Only Barnaby, Peter Pannishly, remains forever young, forever fascinated by the celebrated people he continues to meet.

I, too, am a name dropper, of course. Having written a daily newspaper column since 1938, I know the value of a well-known name and savor as much as Barnaby an anecdote to dine out on for the next several weeks. In one of my earliest columns, I wrote about a handsome teen-aged San Franciscan, the scion of a prominent family, who had stowed away aboard a liner bound for Hawaii and caused something of an international stir when he was discovered hiding in a lifeboat. It was Barnaby Conrad, about whom I have written dozens of items through the long years.

I say in all modesty that I played a small part in making Barnaby a celebrity whose name is being dropped somewhere at this very moment by a nobody seeking to become a somebody.

— Herb Caen, San Francisco
April, 1994

Introduction

The red leather album sits on the cocktail table in our living room. It is the guest book of El Matador, the San Francisco saloon—or was it a salon?—that I created in 1953 and owned for more than a decade. I pick up the book for the first time in a long time and open its pages, which give off a whiff of gin, smoke, and nostalgia. In it is the story of an extraordinary time in the nightlife of San Francisco.

San Francisco has a long history of elegant cafes, raucous restaurants, and colorful cabarets; in its day, El Matador was the most frequented saloon in the salooniest city in the world.

In Laurie Harper's book about Don Sherwood called *The World's Greatest Disc Jockey*, she quotes man-about-town and boss of the popular San Francisco radio station KGO, Russ Coughlan:

> The city had a lot of little clubs with good acts. Barnaby Conrad's place on Broadway was great. He was a wild bastard!
>
> We didn't do dope, we did booze. We dressed in shirts and ties, and had decent haircuts—we weren't going for the absurdity then like now.

> It was a really good time in San Francisco. It was
> before the sleaze. You could walk at night and not get
> killed. It was a town of class . . . San Franciscans saw
> themselves as special, much more so than now.

The fifties were an incredible epoch in San Francisco,
a golden age for cabaret and nightlife in the Barbary
Coast and North Beach areas. Fifty feet east from the Matador on Broadway was Ann's 440 Club, where Johnny
Mathis was discovered. Across the street was the Swiss-
American Hotel where Lenny Bruce, thinking he was a
bird, decided to fly out of a second-story window with
nonfatal if predictable results. A couple of blocks south at
599 Jackson Street, Enrico Banducci's Hungry i welcomed
newcomers Mike Nichols and Elaine May, Woody Allen,
Bill Cosby, the Kingston Trio, the Smothers Brothers,
Jonathan Winters, Mort Sahl, and a completely unknown
singer named Barbra Streisand. (Of the latter, I remember
Banducci urging me, "You just gotta see this incredible
dame—nose like a trombone, voice like an angel!") In one
small nearby section to the west were great little places
like Tosca Café, the Bodega, 12 Adler Place, the Black Cat,
and the Purple Onion. Dapper Henri Lenoir, in his trademark beret, greeted everyone in front of his Vesuvio Café,
whose large sign above the door read, "We Are Itching To
Get Away From Portland, Oregon." The whole area was
jumping, it was safe, and it was gay in the antiquated
sense of the word.

I leaf through the album now, the pages still redolent
of tobacco smoke after more than thirty years. By and
large, it is filled with the banalities that most of us come
up with for guest books. The famous, the once-famous,
and the now-forgotten graciously signed the book during
those three thousand plus nights, but the drawings—lots
of drawings—catch one's eye. For some reason, many of
the people we invited to sign the book felt inspired to do a

picture of some sort, often with a bullfighting motif. A few—like Peter Hurd, Charles Addams, John Falter, and Dong Kingman—were professional artists, but most had no training. ("How long have you been drawing?" "Why, *all evening!*")

This self-portrait by Danny Kaye is a good example. I remember his telling me as he sketched it late one night that not only was this his first drawing but it was the first time he'd signed his real name—David Daniel Kaminski—since he'd changed it so many years ago.

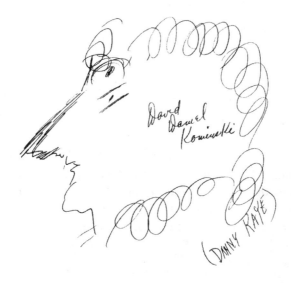

I flip the page to Peter Ustinov's contribution, and once again I hear his deep voice and his marvelous reminiscences as he drew: "Laughton, yes, good old Charles, he was always standing around waiting to be offended. I remember him in the swimming pool. Quite a sight, you can imagine. He was the opposite of an iceberg—nine-tenths of him was visible. Appalling!"

/ Encantado !

Pedro Ustinov

suy ame 4

[Pedro Ustinov)

Hoagy Carmichael drew the first bars of his composition "Stardust," which has been called the most popular song of all time. (Later, Dave Raksin did the same with the opening bars of the runner-up, his song "Laura.")

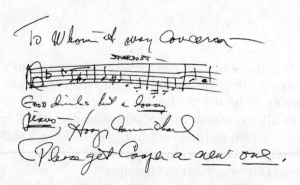

To Whom it may Concern —

Good drinks but a lousy piano — Hoagy Carmichael

(Please get Cooper a *new one*.

That Jonathan Winters's cartoon is expert and professional is no accident—the comedian studied art in Ohio before he became famous in the theatrical world. (He is also an author and is currently working on a book tentatively called *I Couldn't Wait for Success so I Went On Ahead Without It*. It is his autobiography, and not long ago his publisher expressed disappointment that the manuscript didn't contain some lurid anecdotes. "What about your affairs?" wired the publisher. Jonathan shot back simply: "They're in order.")

Here is another guest book entry, a lovely matador drawn by famed painter Robert Watson:

Not every famous person who came in to my place and signed the book did a drawing. Ronald and Nancy Reagan chose not to, as did Judy Garland, Hedda Hopper, and Helen Hayes, who all signed the same page and contented themselves with innocuous little compliments.

I note the surprisingly prim and proper entry by gangster Mickey Cohen, who had just been released from Alcatraz. I recall him agonizing over the unaccustomed and unexpected task, writing slowly, checking each word with his two henchmen: "It is a pleasure to know you and to visit your little club." Sure, El Matador must have seemed "little" to him—he was used to big, flashy joints with floor shows, like the Copacabana in New York and the gaudy Las Vegas clubs. On the way out he rasped: "Hey, people's always talkin' about my henchmen dis and my henchmen dat—I ask you just what da hell *is* a henchman?" I didn't have a ready answer for him.

On the page following Mickey Cohen's greeting is a fine drawing of a bull, standing smug and triumphant in the arena, one horn bloody and a matador's ear at his feet. "This one's human," the caption says. Charles Addams, the famed *New Yorker* cartoonist who was the creator of the Addams Family, said, "I have to label it because I can't draw a realistic ear for sour apples!"

A week later, José Ferrer came into the Matador and chuckled when he saw Addams's cartoon. He drew a bull-fighter resembling himself, with a bloody and dripping ear, connected the drawing to Addams's with an arrow, and captioned it, "And it ain't Van Gogh."

Charlton Heston, an avid sketcher, did a spirited drawing of a cape pass:

John Falter, who created some 120 covers for the *Saturday Evening Post* and whom Norman Rockwell called "America's most gifted illustrator," did this hasty little drawing on the opening night of El Matador. The person in the bullfighting costume is me, seated at a table where a bull's head roast is being carved. Falter spent only a few minutes sketching, but he caught the look of the place—guitar and capes on the wall, votive candles smoldering on a pillar, even one of our macaws perched on a waiter's shoulder.

How did El Matador come to be in the first place? How did this saloon, which attracted so many people, famous and otherwise, and which in retrospect seems to have embodied a San Francisco that is gone forever, get its start?

It began with *Matador*, a novel I wrote in 1952. The book was based on the glorious and tragic life of Spanish bullfighter Manuel Rodríguez, "Manolete," Spain's greatest hero. I came to know him when I was the American vice-consul in Sevilla and Malaga, Spain. On August 28, 1947, this multimillionaire and a bull killed each other and plunged an entire nation into deep mourning. In 1952, I took the basic facts, condensed the action into a fictional twelve hours, and created a surprise—especially to me—blockbuster that was on the best-seller list for a year, was sold to John Huston for a film, and was picked by John Steinbeck as his favorite book of the year. Money, an unfamiliar commodity to me, began rolling in in great increments. What to do with it all?

In 1953, Paul Brooks, the head of Boston-based Houghton Mifflin, which had published *Matador*, came to San Francisco, and we met in a restaurant to discuss my next book. After dinner, he remarked that he'd like to go to "an attractive bar and listen to a good piano." I had to answer that there was no such bar in San Francisco. "Why don't you start one?" he said, half seriously.

That night, I lay awake thinking about his suggestion. I personally found most bars and nightclubs garish and uninviting. Why not open a truly chic and comfortable one, a place where attractive and interesting people could congregate over a martini? I think I also had a deeper motive: I was not happy in my marriage at that time, and I secretly hoped that the girl of my dreams—like Ingrid Bergman in "Casablanca"—would come in. I would look at her and say, "Of all the gin mills in all the cities in all the world, you happened to pick mine." The fact that she did, eventually, is a later, much later, chapter.

The next day I took $35,000 of the money the novel had made, bought an old Mexican dance hall near the Barbary Coast district, and with my friend and fellow writer Niels Mortensen, I began turning it into an elegant bar with a torero motif. We put original Goya etchings (given to me when I was the vice-consul in Sevilla) and beautiful bullfighting costumes and capes on the walls. We even had a genuine Picasso lithograph of a taurine scene displayed prominently. (Some months later a little old lady tottered in and asked a new and uninformed bartender, "Young man, where's the Picasso?" And he replied, "First door to da left, lady.") We designed a fine piano bar—probably the first piano bar in the world—with stools around a baby grand. We set a large glass cage in the wall for four spectacular macaws. Within six weeks the place was transformed, and we were almost ready to open.

Then something unforeseen happened. I was painting away, desperately trying to finish El Matador's huge mural before our big opening, when a swarthy and furtive little man carrying a large box approached. He said he'd heard that I liked unusual pets. He put the box on the bar, and when he slid the lid off, out stepped what was unquestionably the most magnificent bird I had ever seen, a giant, iridescent blue macaw. The creature—almost four feet long from beak to tail—had a round head and mocking black eyes encircled with bright yellow; it looked like a fantastic design for a bird to be submitted to God for approval.

"Hello there!" the bird said to me, with impeccable diction. "Macgregor here!" Gently, he held out a claw for me to shake, and I swear his great black beak smiled. It was love at first sight, the only bird I had ever seen whose personality could match that of Benito, the parrot I had lost many years before when I was at Yale. (The powers that be in Connecticut had decided that parrots were a health threat, so they confiscated and destroyed him.)

"I've had Macgregor since he fell out of his nest at my feet in the Brazilian jungle," said the man, looking over his shoulder uneasily. "He's just like a brudder to me. He's the only hyacinthine macaw in America, wort' at least twelve hunnert, but I'll let you have him for eight hunnert 'n' fifty."

Attributing the man's nervousness to his reluctance to part with his pet, I quickly wrote out a check before he could change his mind. The man patted his "brudder" a hasty good-bye and departed. A few days later, while I was painting the mural, an official-looking man in a trench coat came in and ordered me down from the scaffold. He showed me his FBI credentials, pointed at Macgregor, who was happily swinging from one horn of a mounted bull's head, and explained the bird's true origin. It seemed I had dealt with Rodzima, the head of a small gang that had smuggled an incredible half-million-dollars worth of parrots and macaws into the country from South America the previous year. To get their wares past the guards along the Mexican border, the gang anesthetized the birds and put them in special compartments under the floor-boards of trucks or in clever false trays under chicken crates. Because of the beauty and rarity of the birds, the Brazilian government would not let them out of the country. They had to be smuggled over at least three borders. Once in the States, pet shops and zoos eagerly bought the rare birds. The FBI man assured me that Macgregor was indeed worth about twelve hundred dollars. Rodzima had known that the FBI was closing in on him, so he had come to me rather than risk going to more lucrative markets.

"It's legal to have parrots once they're in California," said the FBI man, "but not if we know how and where they were smuggled in. We marked your macaw with in-frared ink before it even left Brazil, and we've been on its trail ever since. Got to confiscate it."

I had a sick feeling in my stomach.

"Don't look so sad," he said, handing me a subpoena. "We'll let you keep the bird if you show up in court in San Diego on the second of the month, turn State's evidence, and identify Rodzima."

"But that's the day we open this place," I exclaimed. "There are a thousand invitations out, TV cameras, news-papers . . . "

"Then it's bye-bye birdie," he said, turning to leave.

"Wait," I said. "I'll be there!"

The day I flew with Macgregor to San Diego, six hundred miles away, the life-size painting of Manolete was framed and up on the wall of El Matador, but the thirty-by-thirteen-foot mural of the Sevilla bull ring was only half finished, even though Niels had been painting frantically on one side and I on the other. Nevertheless, I made a grand courtroom entrance that day, with the macaw on my shoulder, so that the jurors could finally comprehend why people paid such prices for the birds and how the smugglers had turned their efforts into a half-million-dollar-a-year industry. Once on the stand, Macgregor created

WON'T TALK: Two key witnesses in the San Diego, Calif., federal trial of nine persons charged with smuggling parrots into the U.S. are Baraby Conrad, a San Francisco, Calif., artist, and his bird, MacGregor. Conrad claims he purchased the $1,200 macaw from one of the defendants. MacGregor, being an illegal alien, stood on his constitutional rights and refused to talk.

havoc by flying to the judge's bench and, with the gavel in his beak, imitating the judge's pounding. Then, when I was asked to identify Rodzima as the man who had sold me the bird, I picked out an innocent witness for the State by mistake. There was a hubbub in the courtroom.

"Mr. Conrad forgot his glasses," said the lawyer, hastily handing me his and hissing, "The defendants are over there!"

I finally fingered the right man, the court saw that the smugglers got five years, the FBI gave me permanent custody of Macgregor, and I flew back to San Francisco, arriving two hours before the opening of El Matador.

When people started coming through the door, the liquor hadn't even arrived, and I was still up on a ladder trying to finish the mural. But El Matador was an instant hit. A New York columnist quoted Bennett Cerf, the famous publisher, calling it "the most attractive room in America," which instantly sent droves of tourists to us.

Herb Caen's column in the *San Francisco Chronicle* solidified the success a few days later.

THE GLITTERBUG SET: Mr. Barnaby Conrad, the young man of many talents, opened his new bistro, El Matador, on North Beach's Broadway last Thurs. night—and I'm afraid the garlicky old boulevard of long-haired men and short-haired women will never be the same.

Mr. Conrad's establishment is, to overwork that overworked word, swank. It has wall-to-wall carpets. A bull's head over the bar. A glass aviary containing huge Caen-beaked parrots that look more ferocious than the bull. All kinds of bullfight paintings, including an original by Picasso and several aboriginals by Conrad. A blonde hatchick who's the smoothest thing seen on B'way since they removed the streetcar tracks. And, in a corner, Mr. John Cooper, the eminent saloon pianist, playing smoky melodies.

The opening night was every bit as elegant as the closing night of the opera. Doorman Bob Brown of

Saks, the latter-day Joe Foreman of Shreve's, opened
the car doors. All the belles were there, from Countess
Francesca Latini (oh) to Joan Quigley (ah). [Author's
note: Joan Quigley would become Nancy Reagan's as-
trologer thirty odd—very odd—years later.] Charles O'-
Gara presented Mr. Conrad with a pair of freshly cut
bull's ears, and where he got 'em, the SPCA will never
know. A poodle arrived with Peter Hately. Dan London
paid for his drinks. Everybody else assumed they were
on the house until Mr. Conrad leaped desperately atop
the Steinway—olé!—to announce in a stricken voice
that "'Operation Free Load' is now over. From now on,
the house makes money." Only a few people left, but I
shall return.

The waitress at El Matador is a dark-eyed girl
named Olga Benavides, niece of an ex-president of
Peru, who has been here only two months and speaks
no English. Her job consisted of passing a plate containing French-fried squid—the English word for
which, she was told by some card, is worms. "Worms?"
she kept asking as she made her way through the
throng, "Worms?"

Aside from that, everything went like clockwork
except the clock, which arrived at 2 A.M. before Mr.
Conrad's well-wishers were ready to leave. So Barnaby
called the cops to put an official end to the evening. But
El Matador, I'm happy to say, is here to stay.

In the beginning, people came because the Matador
was a pleasant place to go before or after dinner, and then
as it increased in popularity they came to look at the
celebrities. One never was quite sure who would be in El
Matador: One night we hosted the unlikely potpourri of
Noel Coward, Henry Fonda, Marilyn Monroe, and champion bronc rider Casey Tibbs (none of whom were together). Another time, Sinatra, Hermione Gingold, Zsa
Zsa Gabor, and William Randolph Hearst, Jr., all appeared
on the same evening. Tyrone Power walked in one day

and drank to the mounted bull's head, which came from his film *Blood and Sand*. When I admired his handsome gold cuff links, he sent them to me the next day. People did things like that in those days.

I used to look forward to going to the club in the evenings, seeing old friends and meeting new ones. We had an excellent piano player, the charismatic John Horton Cooper, who was hired at the very beginning and stayed for ten years; he had great musical taste, an unflappable disposition, and his inevitable reaction to any situation or statement—"one never knows, do one?"—became a watchword around North Beach and the Barbary Coast. I enjoyed relieving John every once in a while, secure in the knowledge that no one could fire me. I love playing—what might most charitably be termed "fraternity piano"—and had even enjoyed a two-month stint playing in the Bolivar Hotel nightclub in Lima, Peru, when I was twenty-four. Some nights, while filling in on Johnny's breaks, backed up by our great bassist, Vernon Alley, I would achieve a sublime mediocrity on a tune like "Stardust" or "Smoke Gets in Your Eyes." Vern, a consummate musician, would patiently try to keep me on the beat and give me sage advice, such as when I once hit a wrong chord and stopped to correct it. "Now you've made two mistakes, man! When you hit a clinker, don't then stop to insult the rhythm as well!"

One night I was playing "Body and Soul," an arrangement that I had learned from a teacher in San Mateo, California, at the age of fourteen, when a large figure in an aloha shirt came through the cocktailers to the piano. I recognized him from TV as Merv Griffin. He had an incredulous look on his face as he sat on the bench next to me. He deftly picked up where I was in the piece and played along with me, note by note, chord by chord. It was uncanny.

"You must have taken lessons from Keith Evans in San Mateo," he exclaimed. "I learned the same arrangement from him!" When we finished, we had a pleasant drink and discussed our former music teacher. A handsome, affable young man, Keith had married an older woman, the mother of jazz great Cal Tjader. One day, Keith jumped off the Golden Gate Bridge, leaving this cryptic note on his neatly folded sports jacket: "I changed my mind halfway down!"

His body was never found and many people believe he never jumped, that it wasn't in keeping with his personality.

"I've heard he took a powder to South America," Merv said. "Someone told me they saw him playing in a Chilean nightclub." Subsequent to meeting Merv, I have periodically received brief postcards from different exotic countries: "Watch that D minor in the bass!" signed Keith and postmarked Rio. "Studying the language!" signed Keith and postmarked Bangkok. And most recently: "Down under here working on aboriginal music!" initialed "K.E." and postmarked Sydney, Australia.

I'd like to think these are really from Keith, but on the other hand, Merv travels a lot.

Immortal musicians such as Fatha Hines, Joey Bushkin, Duke Ellington, Erroll Garner, Art Tatum, Teddy Wilson, George Shearing, and André Previn enjoyed stopping by El Matador and playing the piano for fun, and I listened to them with awe.

There was a great sense of camaraderie and fun about the place—and lots of tomfoolery, such as the time a drunk at the end of the bar thought he saw the bull's head on the wall breathe.

"Hey," cried the inebriate, pointing a wavering finger at the bull. "Tha' damned thing's alive!"

He didn't know that some months before we had run a thin hose from the end of the bar down the length of the kitchen, through the walls, and into the great hollow head of the bull to the nostrils. John Clarke, the maître d', would blow a little smoke into his end of the hose from time to time—not too much, mind you—just enough to keep the drunk thinking he was losing his mind.

"Hey, barten'er, there it goes again," he gasped. "Looka tha' damn animal. 'S'breathin'!"

Bill Edison, the gentle bartender, a recent *summa cum laude* graduate from Amherst, pulled himself away from a conversation with sculptor Benny Bufano, adjusted his thick glasses, studied the bull's head solemnly, and announced in his quiet, scholarly way, "Really, sir, I see nothing out of the ordinary, simply a splendid example of a *Piedras Negras toro bravo,* reasonably well taxidermed."

Of course, when Bill turned away, another wisp of smoke, like a suggestion of ectoplasm, wafted down from the bull's muzzle. The drunk gulped his drink, paid up, and lurched out onto Broadway's teeming sidewalk, pale and shaking his head.

Earlier that week Niels Mortensen had experienced a slight contretemps with one of the waiters. We had thought we knew all the ways that one could be cheated in the bar business, but here was a new wrinkle. We'd been aware for some days that not all of the bar's money was showing up in the till at the end of the evening. We certainly knew the thief wasn't among our faithful bartenders nor our several longtime waiters. For a week we'd had a new waiter, so when Niels heard him gurgle, the jig was up. It seems that the enterprising chap had hung two douche bags around his neck under his shirt; one filled with gin, the other with scotch. The hoses from each ran down his arms under his sleeves. He would get the ice and mixers himself from the end of the bar, spritz his own alcohol into the glass, and eliminate the necessity for a bartender and a cash register altogether. Niels congratulated him on his ingenuity, then firmly booted him out the back door and into the parking lot.

All the people who worked in "The Mat" seemed to be characters. Our accountant, Grace West, was an aging Bohemian who wrote flowery poetry. Jack Negherbon, our janitor, played a mean guitar and raised parrots. Our men's room was entirely covered with blackboard slate, complete with chalk trays, and our graffiti was of high caliber ("Edith Head gives good costume;" and "with lecherous howls I deflower young owls;" etcetera). One day I found that Jack had done a fine chalk drawing. It depicted an arena with the audience made up of bulls and a bull in the ring caping a man. Underneath was the legend, "When the last corrida's over, on the shining sands tomorrow, toros will toreros be, toreros will be toros." I couldn't bear to have it erased so I painted it on for permanence.

The cleaning lady, Viola, was a character, too; once she borrowed a copy of *Lady Chatterly's Lover* from the book rack in the kitchen and left me a note the next day: "Thanks for the book. That Mrs. Chatterly didn't know what she wanted—but she sure knew what she needed!"

Niels took care of business and personnel problems during the day while I wrote and painted portraits in my Telegraph Hill studio. I allowed myself the joy of painting in the afternoon only if I'd written a thousand words in the morning. I had attended special art schools when I was a child and had studied art at Yale, the University of Mexico, and in Paris. Portraits were and are my specialty. I did charcoal portraits, by both commission as well as caprice, of many of the patrons of El Matador over the years, and I include some in the following pages. But, in this book, I'm mostly interested in giving the reader a word picture of some of the characters who stepped into my life and inhabited this small part of San Francisco in the 1950s and early 1960s. Yes, I'm a name dropper, but certainly not the first nor the best.

My inspiration for this book came from an English antiquary named John Aubrey, who lived from 1626 to 1697. Born ten years after Shakespeare's death, he was the champion name dropper of all time. His *Brief Lives* gives a lively, sometimes poignant, sometimes hilarious, and sometimes raunchy picture of many of the prominent people of his time. Here is a typical entry from Aubrey:

> Edw. de Vere
>   This Earle of Oxford, making of his low obeisance
> to Queen Elizabeth, happened to let a Fart at which he
> was so abashed and ashamed that he went to Travell 7
> yeares. On his returne the Queen welcomed him home
> and sayd, My Lord, I had forgott the Fart.

Mr. Aubrey is, admittedly, a tough act to follow, but I shall do my best.

Part One

When I created El Matador, I was living in a little house at 844 Bay Street. As my family grew, we moved to a bigger house on Pacific and then to a house we built across the bay on the lagoon in Belvedere. For years I maintained a ludicrous schedule: I would set forth from home at eight in the morning for the twenty-five-minute trip across the bridge to my studio on Telegraph Hill, write and paint until five, go home to play with my kids and have dinner with my wife, and then return to San Francisco at nine and stay until midnight. It was crazy, but if one had to commute, what a lovely one that was. Every day I looked forward to crossing the bridge and seeing San Francisco shining in the morning light. At the toll station, I enjoyed seeing other drivers and passengers all laughing at the same time—*everybody* listened to disk jockey Don Sherwood in the morning with his tales of Lance Boyle and Luz Morales in his improvised soap opera "Just Plain Rosita," which was "brought to you by Splat, the real man's deodorant—it comes in a bucket an' ya put it on with a trowel." And that laugh of Sherwood's—that dirty, wonderful laugh of his that would send all of us commuters into convulsions! As Herb Caen said, "If you could put Sherwood's laugh into words, it would be unprintable."

Jack Kerouac wrote—so long ago and so well—in *Desolation Angels:*

> It's the bridge that counts, the coming-into-San Francisco . . . over waters which are faintly ruffled by ocean-going Orient ships and ferries, over waters that are like taking you to some other shore. . . . It's seeing the rooftops of Frisco that makes you excited and believe, the big downtown hulk of buildings, Standard Oil's flying red horse, Montgomery Street high buildings, Hotel St. Francis, the hills, magic Telegraph with her Coit-top, magic Russian, magic Nob, and magic Mission beyond with the cross of all sorrows I'd seen long ago in a purple sunset with Cody on a little railroad bridge—San Francisco, North Beach, Chinatown, Market Street, the bars, the Bay-Oom, the Bell Hotel, the wine, the alleys, the poorboys, Third Street, poets, painters, Buddhists, bums, junkies, girls, millionaires, MGs, the whole fabulous movie of San Francisco . . . the tug at your heart.

In 1947, Jack Kerouac came from Lowell, Massachusetts, to the Bay Area and fell in love with San Francisco. He and Allen Ginsberg, Alan Watts, Gregory Corso, Michael McClure, and Lawrence Ferlinghetti helped make North Beach the mecca for the Beat Generation in the mid-1950s.

And, of course, Rexroth. Kenneth Rexroth would hold forth at the Matador reciting poem after poem, sometimes in Japanese, not caring whether we understood or not. Like Rexroth, the novelist Herb Gold straddled the worlds of both the Beats and the Establishment, but offbeat writers like Kerouac and the others usually preferred the atmosphere of, say, the Coffee Gallery, the Co-Existence Bagel Shop, and The Place, all around the corner on Grant Avenue.

Jack Kerouac came into the Matador only one time, and he was already a star. He had an aura about him. His 1957 book, *On the Road,* written, it was claimed, in twenty days, had made a big impression all over America but especially in San Francisco, home of flower children and beatniks (a word, incidentally, coined by columnist Herb Caen). *On the Road* is the wild saga of a group of pals wandering across the continent, boozing, whoring, and "digging the scene." It catalogues the postwar search for meaning with live-for-the-moment intensity, absolute honesty, and a fascination with ethnic subcultures.

> I walked with every muscle aching among the lights of
> 27th and Welton in the Denver colored section, wishing
> I were a Negro, feeling that the best the white world
> had offered was not enough ecstasy for me, not enough
> life, joy, kicks, darkness, music, not enough night. . . .

It was about Kerouac, incidentally, that Truman Capote made his famous and unjustified remark, "That's not writing, that's typing."

Kerouac came into the bar that night with Larry Ferlinghetti, the celebrated poet and owner of City Lights Bookstore. I'd never met the author of *On the Road* before, and actually, I was reluctant to meet him since I'd just written an unfavorable review of his latest book, *Dharma Bums,* which had appeared in the *Saturday Review.* He was tanned, good looking, and a little drunk, but intriguing. I thought he was older than me, and he was, by thirteen days.

"I'm sorry I had to write that review," I said to the beatnik god. "I liked *On the Road* a lot, but I just didn't understand this one."

"You will," he said affably. "In about ten years, you will."

Then his mood changed. He stared sadly into his bourbon, as though the answer to the mystery of life lay among the ice cubes.

"Been readin' Freud," he said. "No man can believe in his own death, Freud says, and when he tries to imagine it, he perceives that he really survives as a spectator. But then, Freud's a fraud. Say that three times fast—Freud's a fraud, Freud's a fraud, Frood's a fried. See, I can't do it."

Then he brightened and clapped me on the shoulder. "You know, life's like a sewer—you get out of it what you put into it."

Without another word, he lurched out into the night, on the road again.

In the fifties, Barbary Coast and North Beach saloon keepers, nightclub owners, and restaurateurs used to visit cordially back and forth. Even ex-madame Sally Stanford would come over from her Sausalito restaurant, Valhalla, with her beloved parrot, Loretta, on her shoulder. We were all friends. Coke Infante of the Condor, Henri Lenoir of Vesuvio, Enrico Banducci of the Hungry i, and others would make the rounds of each other's places—we didn't mind the store *all* the time. I'd take in the wonderful singing waiters and waitresses at the Bocce Ball at least once a week, and when Mike Nichols and Elaine May did their comedy and improv act at the Hungry i for a month, I was there every night. On Sundays, the Black Cat served brunch with opera and fizzes, and the tenor, José, dressed in jeans and high-heeled red shoes, would sing the parts of Carmen, Mimi, and Tosca. (Quipped a customer: "He can also handle men's parts.")

Performers from nearby clubs and shows would come into the Mat between or after performances. Flamboyant Inez Torres would undulate by after dancing at the Sinaloa. Walter Hart, the queen of Finnochio's next door, was a regular, as was Wing, the inscrutable Chinese artist, who was a walking fortune cookie ("Wise is the ax that sharpens itself," and so on). Eartha Kitt, Ronny Graham, Paul Lynde, and their producer, Leonard Silliman, came in nearly every night of the long, long run of their show, *New Faces*.

One evening I said to Leonard, who was preparing a new show, "You really should go down a block to Ann's 440 Club and catch the singer—a kid just out of high school with the damnedest voice you ever heard. Nobody ever sang 'Flamingo' quite like that. Going to be a big star, and they're selling his contract for only five hundred dollars."

Leonard, always looking for new talent, scurried out of the Matador. He came back in an hour looking elated.

"Got him!" he exclaimed.

"You got Johnny Mathis?"

"Naw," said Leonard, "couldn't stand his weird voice. But I signed up the female impersonator on the program, T. C. Jones—going to put him on Broadway next season in a one-man show that I guarantee will be a huge hit!"

He did, and it was.

Another performer from down the street, Lenny Bruce, spent a lot of time at the Matador. I remember that one night he was at the bar nursing a Coke when he saw the flamenco dancer José Greco and his group come in.

"Those flamingo dancers knock me out," he said in his Long Island accent. "The guys always stand there clapping their hands over their heads, lookin' down over one shoulder as though they're applaudin' their own ass."

Labeling Lenny Bruce "irreverent" would be like calling Lizzie Borden unfilial. Steve Allen, another visitor to the Mat, wrote in his book *Funny People:* "There are few people to whom I would apply the word *genius*, but Lenny Bruce is one such. He was certainly a great deal more than just a successful nightclub comedian; he was, in fact, a comic philosopher." One night Lenny and Jonathan Winters came in at the same time. After a brief nod they sat at tables across the room from each other. They were a study in contrasts: Midwestern Jonathan—stocky, jowly, jolly; and New Yorker Lenny—lean, swarthy, and good-looking in a ferrety, furtive way. I'm not sure just how it happened, who started it, but all of a sudden they were both on their feet doing comic routines at each other like dueling banjos while the lucky customers who happened to witness it clutched their sides in helpless laughter. Oh, to have had a tape recorder!

I don't remember everything that happened that night, but Jonathan did a wild reenactment of what Babe Ruth's dressing room might have been like after he hit his sixtieth home run. Something like this, with Jonathan alternately doing the Babe and his manager:

"Babe, there are a lot of kids outside waiting for autographs."

"Screw the kids—where're the broads, the booze?"

"They've been waiting a long time, Babe. Here's some baseballs to autograph for them."

"Oh shit, all right. Hand me the rubber stamp and open the door." (Stamping the balls.) "This is for the skinny little Eye-talian here—what's your name, boy?"

"Joe, sir, Joe DiMaggio."

"There you go, you little fag. And what's that little kid's name next to you?"

"Jackie, sir, Jackie Robinson."

"Well, here's one for you, you little runt."

And so forth, growing more outrageous all the time. Then Lenny would try to top whatever Jonathan had done. One bit of Lenny's involved Oral Roberts getting a collect call from Rome from the newly elected Pope John:

"Hello, Johnny, what's shakin', baby? Yeah, the puff of smoke knocked me out. . . . Got an eight-page layout with Viceroy: 'The New Pope Is a Thinking Man.' . . . Hey, listen, Billy wants to know if you can get him a deal on one of them dago sports cars. . . . When you comin' to the coast? I can get you the Steve Allen show the nineteenth. . . . Wear the big ring. . . . Yeah, sweetie, you cool it, too. . . . No, nobody knows you're Jewish!"

Jonathan countered with Maud Frickert's tale of her brother Maynard's attempt to fly with 146 pigeons Scotch-taped to his arms: "Got airborne, did all right, till those bad boys threw the popcorn on the ground in the quarry . . . " Word began to spread up and down the street about this impromptu comic windfall. People hurried in to catch what they could of the happening.

It was a night to remember, and Lenny was a person to remember. Dustin Hoffman in the film *Lenny*, while relentlessly earnest, failed to show how very funny Lenny was; he wasn't just a dirty-talking civil rights crusader. Of course, he did shock San Francisco at the time—this was in the Eisenhower years when even using the word "virgin" in a movie, which happened in *The Moon Is Blue,* could shake up Hollywood and the nation. People on the stage didn't use such language as a ten-letter word for an oral copulator, nor did they mock formal religion or discuss racial discrimination. But Lenny inspired belly-laugh humor when he discussed serious and controversial matters. One night a Texas redneck in the audience was giving him a bad time about a racial issue. Lenny pointed a finger at him.

"Sir, let me put something to you. You're on a desert island, and you have your choice of marrying a black woman or a white woman, right? Now, before you answer with your choice, I feel obliged to tell you that the black woman is Lena Horne and the white woman is Kate Smith."

Even the victim laughed.

Another time he said, "Look, I don't talk dirty. It's you people who have the dirty minds. For example, give me a four letter word ending in unt meaning a woman." (Pause) "See what I mean? I was thinking of aunt."

Off stage Lenny was shy, gentle, and loving, with a delightful naughty-little-boyness about him. The only time I ever saw him irritated was once when I thoughtlessly telephoned him at eight in the morning.

"I hope I didn't wake you up," I said.

"Oh shit no," came the mumbled growl. "I always get up thirteen hours before I go to work!"

It was terrible to see him shrivel up and lose his health, his humor, and his career after the ordeal of his obscenity trials in San Francisco, Los Angeles, and New York. The New York trial alone lasted almost six months. He always thought he would be found innocent—he believed passionately in the First Amendment—but he was found guilty and faced a long term in jail.

While his case was being appealed, his drug use increased. One night in his room in the Swiss-American Hotel, across the street from the Matador, he ran around his room flapping his arms and shouting, "I'm Super-Jew!" He then leapt from the second-floor window and crashed to the sidewalk. Miraculously, he was not killed, and when the medical emergency crew came to take him to the hospital, they first taped his mouth shut to silence the obscenities he was screaming.

On August 6, 1966, he was found in a hotel bathroom dead of an overdose at the age of forty. Ironically, after his death all his obscenity convictions were reversed.

Toward the end he had told his mother, "I failed at what I tried. I thought I could show them a way to care; instead of feeling hatred, I wanted to wipe out all the hypocrisy. But it's like opera, not everyone likes opera. . . . "

As writer Paul Krassner eulogized him: "He fought for the right to say on the nightclub stage what he had the right to say in his own living room." And Joe Morgenstern wrote in a very perceptive article on him in *Playboy*, "Comics always fail. Failure is written into their contract with a tumultuous world that has more pressing things to do than laugh."

Lenny is still funny, not in print perhaps, but on the few recordings one can still find—comedic classics like "Comic at the Palladium" and "Thank You, Masked Man," his portrait of the Lone Ranger as an insufferable Jewish moralizer. But he left a larger legacy. Very few comics are happy off stage; mixing high ethics and belly laughs is tough on a man's soul, as the sad saga of Lenny Bruce showed us. But in San Francisco, he also demonstrated that someone who dares to speak out, using humor as a scalpel, can change the way we look at ourselves forever.

"He looked like a saloon brawler," someone once said. "But he was a pussycat—he stepped high over bugs." When John Steinbeck came into El Matador for the first time with his vivacious wife, Elaine, he was of course asked to sign our guest book. He thought quite a while and drank several beers before writing the following in Spanish:

Si no quieres volar, cuidado con las alas
Si no quieres luchar —
lo mismo con los Toros —
John Steinbeck
pero si quieres beber, paga ahorita. (Steinbeck)

This translates into: "If you don't want to fly, beware of wings and if you don't want to fight the same goes for bulls. But if you want to drink pay for it right now."

This seemed to make a lot of sense to both of us at the time. Steinbeck meant a lot to me.

That same evening he said they were going to dinner at some small restaurant around the corner because they couldn't get a reservation at Trader Vic's. I was amazed.

"Did you tell Trader Vic's your name?"

Elaine shook her head. "John would never do that."

"What's the point," I said, "of working all your life to be John Steinbeck and then not using it to get a lousy reservation in a restaurant you want to go to?" I called the restaurant, dropped the name, and they went to Trader Vic's for dinner. But that's the kind of self-effacing guy he was.

When a person writes his first best-selling novel, life sort of explodes. It certainly did for me when *Matador* was published in 1952. The first indication that life was going to be different was when my friend Bob, the postman, began calling me "Mister Conrad." Anyone who suddenly received all that mail had to be *very* important. From struggling artist and teacher, I had overnight become an Author with a capital A.

Although the money and the heady reviews and the TV interviews were dazzling, the biggest thrill of all was picking up a copy of the *Saturday Review* in which a dozen titans of literature were asked to pick their favorite book of the year. After John Steinbeck's name was simply: *Matador.*

I dashed off a gushy letter of thanks to the author of *Grapes of Wrath* and *Of Mice and Men,* who, along with Hemingway and Fitzgerald, was my favorite writer. I received this a few days later.

Dear Conrad:
    I like bullfighting. To me it is a lonely, formal, anguished microcosm of what happens to every man, even in an office strangled by the glue on the envelopes. In the bull ring, he manages to survive for a while. Sometimes.

Sincerely,
John

P.S. My wife and I are going to the Virgin Islands next week to watch the fish do it. Care to join us?

Would I? Did I! And what a wonderful week it was.

We became good friends, and saw each other frequently over the years. And when in San Francisco, he would always come into the Matador.

In 1960, I produced and wrote a modest film based on his story "Flight," and he kindly consented to be filmed along the Monterey coast, where the story takes place, and give a little introduction to the film. (This is where I did my portrait of him.) After the filming, we drove through the town of Monterey. He had not been there for twenty-four years, and he was horrified by the changes and the commercialization that had taken place. "Oh, look," said Elaine, his wife. "There's the Steinbeck Theater!" But he was morose, and he wouldn't even stop to look at that tribute to him. As we drove along the shore, Elaine spotted a sea lion working the waves for fish. "That's what I want to be in my next life! What do you want to be, Barny?" I said I thought a hawk's life would be nice. "How about you, John?" she asked cheerily.

"I want to be a bug," John growled.

"A bug?"

"A chocolate-flavored bug."

Elaine looked at him bemusedly. "A choc—"

"Doc—Ed Ricketts!" Steinbeck interrupted. "He once tasted a chocolate-flavored bug. Just once. Could never find another like it."

I naively asked, "Did Doc Ricketts go around eating bugs?"

Steinbeck gave me a withering glance. "I didn't say he *ate* the bug! He just tasted it as any true scientist would." He shook his head. "He never could find another one that exact flavor. I'd like to be that bug for him in the next life."

I recently had a postcard from John's widow saying simply, "I miss the chocolate-flavored bug."

When the feature-length film *Flight* was finally finished, it seemed amateurish, since most of us connected with it were new to filmmaking, and it was done on a shoestring. But it had an art house feel to it, the California scenery was beautiful, and the young Mexican who played the fugitive killer was convincing. To our amazement, it was chosen at the last minute to open the Edinburgh Film Festival, one of the best in Europe.

I was making arrangements to fly the next day to Scotland with the film when someone pointed out that there was a clause in Steinbeck's contract stating that the author had to see and approve of the film before it could be shown anywhere.

In a panic I telephoned Steinbeck in Sag Harbor, Long Island. Could he possibly see the film the next day during my stopover in Manhattan on my way to Scotland? No. He wasn't well enough to come in to New York, but there was a little theater in Sag Harbor if I would bring the film there. I arrived the next morning in New York, and since the only train had left for Sag Harbor, I took a hundred-dollar taxi ride to the theater where the bearlike Steinbeck and his wife awaited me. The three of us sat alone as the theater went dark and the film began. For an hour he didn't say a word, only sighing occasionally as he watched the creatures of his imagination flit across the screen. I squirmed and kept sneaking looks at his goateed face, trying to gauge what the occasional frown or neck tugging portended. How childish my dialogue suddenly sounded, how amateurish the acting. Finally, as he watched a tight close-up of the wounded, fleeing, frightened Mexican boy creep slowly around the weather-beaten boards of a deserted shack, Steinbeck cleared his throat. He cleared it again. I tensed. He leaned over to me, and I eagerly leaned toward him. He patted my arm.

"Good texture," he rasped, "good wood texture."

I sank back into my seat. Wouldn't that look great on the theater marquees: "Steinbeck says, 'Good Wood Texture.'" I sweated out the final twenty minutes. The lights came on. We left the theater and drove in silence to the

Steinbecks' rambling house. John immediately retired to his study.

"How did he like it?" I whispered to Elaine.

She shrugged sympathetically. "Who knows?"

A few moments later, Steinbeck appeared and handed me a piece of paper. It read: "This film has tremendous quality, great simplicity of approach, and I found it moving—deeply moving." He broke out the champagne, and we toasted happily to wood texture. The movie received fine reviews at Edinburgh and at the London film festival. In fact, it is still shown today at festivals and universities around the world.

John knew a lot about bullfighting. He told me a good story about Mario Cabré. This once-handsome Barcelona bullfighter gave the word *dilettante* new meaning. Although a full matador, he was also a playwright, poet, novelist, and actor, *The Flying Dutchman* being his best-known film. He was also the longtime lover of Ava Gardner.

Perhaps because of his well-publicized amatory adventures and his various literary pursuits, Cabré was never taken very seriously by his bullfighting peers. John Steinbeck had seen him fight once in Barcelona against a dangerous animal.

"He got himself in a compromising position, thought flight the better part of valor, headed for the fence, and dove over it headfirst. In doing so, the point of the sword nicked a veteran banderillero's arm."

The old man looked in amazement as his arm started to bleed, and as they led him away to the infirmary, Steinbeck heard the man growl, "Been in this business for thirty years, and this is the first time I've ever been wounded by a *poet!*"

Steinbeck added that the amount of *desprecio,* or loathing, with which the banderillero infused the word *poet* was remarkable.

Steinbeck told me that he once sat next to a little man at the bullfights during the entire week of the annual

Feria of Sevilla. He said, "He was a nice little man in a business suit who very considerate and knowledgeably explained everything that was going on. I never enjoyed bullfighting so much. Only after we left the city did I find out he was Juan Belmonte, the greatest bullfighter of all."

I wonder if Belmonte ever found out who *he'd* been sitting next to!

I treasure the last time I saw John Steinbeck. We met in San Francisco while he was on the final lap of driving his camper around the United States, the basis of his best-selling book *Travels with Charley.* We were at Enrico's sidewalk café, and Charley, the big black poodle, sat obediently in a corner near our table. With us was Howard Gossage, the innovative advertising man, who among other things had given the world the current rage, Beethoven sweatshirts. Oh, to have had a tape recorder and been able to catch the sound as well as the words of the following dialogue, because John growled out his sentences in unique ursine grunts while Howard's congenital stammer heightened rather than hampered his wit.

"Look at that dog over there," said John. "Yesterday in the great redwoods of Muir Woods he lifted his leg on a tree that was twenty feet across, a hundred feet high, and a thousand years old. Howard, Howard! What's left in life for that poor dog?"

Howard thought of the terrible dilemma for a moment and then said, "Well, J-J-John, he could always t-t-teach!"

Though one of the funniest men alive, Jonathan Winters never tells jokes. He describes people in situations, usually thought up on the spot and rarely repeated the same way.

Once in the Matador I heard a friend at the bar challenge him: "All right, Jonathan, you're a six-year-old boy asking a seven-year-old girl for a date."

Without missing a beat, the ex-marine went into a childish fidgety slouch and, playing both parts, said shyly, "Yer the new girl, aren't you."

"Yes." A little stand-offish. "My name is Deedee."

"I've got a goldfish named Ralph."

"You do?"

"He'th my friend. Wanna thee him?"

Deedee, skeptically, "Where is he?"

"In my pocket." Takes out fish and looks at him tenderly. "Thee, hith eyeth are clothed. He'th athleep right now. Would you like to go to the movieth with me tonight?"

"Yes."

"What time shall I come to your houth?"

"Oh," little girl, airily, "Sevenish."

Jonathan and I first met in 1956, when, between his unforgettable performances at the renowned Hungry i cabaret down the street, the great comic would unwind for an hour or so at El Matador, a bull in search of a china shop. In those days, Jonathan drank a bit, and he liked to have a couple as he listened to the pianist after one of his brilliant, improvisational shows. Over the years, we've become good friends, and we have remained so in spite of his phone calls—that's right, in spite of. The first in what has become a long series went like this:

In Oxfordian and veddy wealthy tones: "Hellooo, is Bahneby theh?"

My wife, Mary: "I'm sorry, he's gone to the post office."

"Pity! Temby here, Edward Temby." A brief, humble hesitation. "Lord Temby, echtchooly. I was so hoping to talk to the old darling—knew him in Spain yez and yez ago. I believe, Mrs. Conrad, that . . . "

"Please, call me Mary." (I should add that Mary is quite impressed with royalty, genuflecting the day she met Duke Ellington, for example.)

"Mary, yes, of course, Teddy here. I believe you know the Mellons, right, Mary?"

The only melons we knew were honeydew, Persian, and cantaloupe, but Mary found herself saying, "I think maybe I went to school with some."

"I must say, Mary dear," continued Lord Temby, "that you sound teddibly attractive." Then suddenly lecherously, "I say, what if I pop down there, and we go to the beach and go skinny dipping?"

And the jig was up.

"Jonathan!"

Since then he has fooled us dozens of times with a variety of voices. But then one never knows when he is going to strike or for sure just who it is on the other end. Once he was Jamey Wyeth, "a friend of your publisher who said to look you up on my way through town." Jonathan made it sound totally plausible, and since I've always wanted to meet the talented artist, I invited him to our house. I didn't know it was a deception until his farewell line: "We're here at the hotel, so I'll jump on Argyll first and then we'll toodle down in about ten minutes."

From time to time there are the messages we find on the answering machine: "Hello, you old darlings," he began in a Locust Valley, investment banker lockjaw accent. "It's Binky, Binky Hamilton! Listen, you two old sweethearts, mother's dead. Yes, we found her this morning face down in the trout stream, but the good news is she's left you some flat silver worth about $40,000, so fond of you two darlings. Damn good pattern, you'll see. Ta-ta!"

Or another time:

"Hi!" He began with a long, drawn-out, soulful "hi" that sounded more like *hahyeee*. "It's Bruce? Bruce at White Cygnet Antiques? And say, lissen guys, I hate to be the one to tell you but you know that Limoges vase you brought in? Virgil says it's a flaming fake and you just can't trust the Paris flea market anymore."

When the situation is reversed and one calls the Winters's residence, there's no telling what will transpire. Sometimes he answers in his wife's voice and says, "Oh, dear, no, he's not here. They came and got him some time ago, those nice men in white. One of them was fresh with me, too, snapped my bra . . . "

Once he answered in a gravelly San Quentin growl, saying: "They is out. We're just robbin' the joint—hey Steve, easy wit dat TV set . . . "

Not even bilingual wrong numbers are safe from Jonathan. One midnight a man woke him up saying, *"Luis? Quiero hablar con Luis!"*

"You have the wrong number, my friend," said Jonathan politely. But two minutes later the man called back.

"Luis? Luis? Está mi amigo Luis?"

"No," intoned Jonathan sadly. *"Luis está muerto,"* he said and hung up.

His boyhood companions are often his telephonic victims. Sometimes on Christmas trips to his hometown of Springfield, Ohio, Jonathan would call up some of his high school classmates. One was Art Lytle, who had become a funeral director. Putting on his finely honed Ozark accent Jonathan said:

"Jackson-Lytle Funeral Home? This is Lamar Gene Gumbody, an' say lissen, my stepbrother died here Sunday week an' we're out here on Route 4 an' we was wonderin' if you people could come out an' get him?"

"Uh—when did you say he died?"

"Sunday week."

"Good god man, where've you got him?"

"Well, we moved him out on the porch an' set him up there against the lattice an' the cold spell that we had froze him harder'n a carp. Then the weather turned warm an' he kinda went fleshy on us; his face dropped an' all. My oldest boy said there's humor even in death an' he twisted the deceased's hand around an' put a softball in his fist."

About that time, the funeral director caught on.

"Jonathan Winters," he said sadly. "You were an ass in high school and you're an ass now."

These days, running the Santa Barbara Writers' Conference makes us target for some unusual calls, but over the years Mary and I have become wary, and when someone named Professor Lawrence Hoggins Olmstead calls us at writers' conference time and wants to speak on "sexual dysfunction in twentieth-century literature," or someone says he's an ex-student and has finally finished that epic saga about Patagonian sheepherders ("But you promised,"—(wailing)—"you *promised* to read it!"), it only takes us a few minutes to figure out that it is the Mad Man of Romero Canyon at work again. But sometimes the detector breaks down.

Last month an ancient, quavery Grandma Frickert voice inquired, "Mr. Conrad, this is Mabel Jane Pemberton calling long distance from San Francisco." The line crackled and I visualized Jonathan blowing on the mouthpiece to validate the long distance element. "My husband is Willis P. Pemberton, you know, the librarian at the public library for so many years? And I was wondering how much you would charge to write his exciting life story, such a fascinating life and a wealth of material—"

"Jonathan," I interrupted, "you're slipping." He wasn't going to catch me this time.

"Beg pardon?"

"That's not even a good Frickert. It stinks."

"Mr. Conrad," said the old voice. "I took your class at Marina High adult education forty years ago, and you needn't be rude to me!"

It dawned on me with a rush—Jonathan couldn't have known about that brief teaching stint. I began my abject apology to a bewildered Mrs. Willis Pemberton, already imagining Jonathan's gleeful cackle when I told him this story.

Frank Sinatra's entry in the guest album of El Matador is signed simply, "The Leader." The novelist William Kennedy wrote about attending a Sinatra concert: "A lifetime of staying young at center stage: how can anybody be so good for so long? . . . You follow him with your eyes because he is carrying the sound of your youth, the songs of your middle age. And then you think, the song is you, pal, the song is you."

I first met him in Springfield, Ohio, when I was seventeen, and he had just joined Harry James's band. He was an unknown young man with big ears who appeared almost tubercular and who clung to the mike stand as though for support. I was visiting my prep school roommate, and this was the town's big charity ball. Sinatra, who was repeatedly called "Sintra" all night, was charming to us kids in between songs. We all predicted he'd be famous one day, which happened about six months later when he and Tommy Dorsey recorded, among other classics, "I'll Never Smile Again."

In the fifty years since, I've only seen him half a dozen times, and he's always been the perfect gentleman. In my saloon, he would chat with strangers or sign autographs cheerfully, even when his conversation or serious drinking was being interrupted.

One night in El Matador, I was sitting at a table with the mercurial Mr. Sinatra and some of his cronies when a tall and elegantly dressed Englishwoman approached and shyly asked for his autograph.

"Sure, Baby," the singer said, adding with a leer in Sinatra-ese, "And how's your bird?"

"I-I don't have a bird," she stammered.

"Oh, lady," cracked Sinatra, "then you're in deep trouble!"

His toadies guffawed, and the woman reddened. Confused, she started to retreat. The other Sinatra came to the fore: realizing he had embarrassed her, he jumped up, grabbed a chair from a nearby table, and insisted she join him for champagne. She left mollified and dazzled half an hour later.

Another night Herb Caen took me up to Sinatra's suite at the Fairmont Hotel. A steady stream of people came through, and Frank insisted on making the drinks for them all, from eleven at night till five in the morning. There was caviar and champagne, and the music on the elaborate sound system was exclusively Sinatra. Frank sang along with himself and drank steadily, not champagne, only bourbon, without apparent effect. When a doctor asked him once how much he drank, Frank answered, "Thirty-six drinks a day—that's how many in a bottle of Jack Daniels."

"Good Lord, you must feel terrible in the morning," said the doctor.

"I don't know," Frank replied. "I'm never up in the morning."

He was polite and attentive this particular evening, making sure everyone was happy. Around two o'clock, one of the publicity men, well taken with wine, misguidedly decided to tell an anecdote he'd heard to a group in a corner of the suite:

"Once when Frank and Ava were in Africa on location, they were introduced to an important official. John Ford, the director, for some reason, said, 'Ava, honey, why don't you tell the governor here what you see in this one-hundred-and-twenty-pound runt you're married to?' Ava didn't lose any of her cool, just said, 'Well, there's only ten pounds of Frank, but there's one hundred and ten pounds of cock!'"

There was dead silence in the suite as the man finished the story and people looked over at Frank to see whether they should laugh or not. A glance at Sinatra's fierce and dark scowl told them. He put down his glass and started slowly across the room, his fists clenched. The miscreant, twice Sinatra's size, turned and fled, Frank kicking him in the stern repeatedly as he stumbled out of the door. Then Sinatra turned back to the group and, smiling, said, "Let's all raise a toast to Ava."

I had a strange last encounter with Sinatra. He was having a bad time in his relationship with Ava Gardner, who was enjoying a much-publicized affair with the matador Luis Miguel Domínguín in Spain. Domínguín had been the immortal Manolete's biggest rival until the latter's death in the arena. Sinatra was rumored to be close to suicide in his anger and jealous frustration.

One day Frank called Herb Caen from Hollywood and said, "Set up a meeting with Barnaby Conrad for tomorrow." The three of us met in a Sausalito restaurant, and as we made small talk through lunch, Frank was his most charming and expansive. Over coffee, Frank suddenly produced a manila envelope and took out a dozen large photos.

"What do you think of these?" he said, holding them up almost shyly. They were pictures of himself dressed as a matador in a beautiful "suit of lights." "Had it tailored special," he said proudly. He was made up to look like Manolete, with a big nose and the gray streak in his hair. "Not bad, huh?"

Then he said. "I want to buy the rights to your book *Matador.*"

"Great," I said. The picture of him in a matador's hat made him look a little like a Mouseketeer.

"We'll film it in Spain," he said.

"Great," I said. I could speak Hollywoodese with the best of them.

"A big, *big* movie," he said. "Authentic."

"Great," I said.

"Not bad, eh?" he said. "I look pretty good here, don't I?"

"Great," I said.

"My people and I will call you tomorrow about the rights," he said.

"Great," I said.

We shook hands, left the place, and I never saw or heard from him again. Not long afterward, I read in a gossip column that Ava Gardner had broken up with Domínguín; apparently that also broke up Sinatra's brief love affair with *la fiesta brava.*

Marilyn Monroe came into the Matador with a gentleman who was neither Joe DiMaggio nor Arthur Miller nor a Kennedy. He signed the guest book "Peter Lawford," but she, in a scarf and dark glasses, declined to sign. Marilyn asked Johnny Cooper, the piano player, for "Laura." They finished their drinks and left before I arrived. I didn't meet her until a year later, when I joined producer Arthur P. Jacobs for lunch at 20th Century Fox. Jacobs (*Planet of the Apes, Doctor Doolittle,* and so on) had taken an option on my novel *Matador* and wanted to discuss the making of it. But after I arrived, some minor studio crisis required his attention.

"This will take about an hour," he said apologetically, escorting me out of his office. "If you don't mind, I'll park you in the rehearsal room. Might amuse you. Jack Cole is teaching Marilyn Monroe a new routine for her next picture."

He led me into a long, bare room lined with mirrors. A wiry man in tights, shaved bald, with a raptor nose was executing a complicated dance step while Marilyn watched. "Got it?" he panted.

"Well," she said, uncertainly. "Maybe."

Arthur introduced me, then retreated. Marilyn nodded shyly but didn't speak; I was immediately reminded of Steinbeck's girl from *Cannery Row,* the "sturdy blonde who mistrusted language as a means of communication." Then Cole turned up the volume on the dance music and ordered, "And a six, seven, eight . . . "

For over an hour I watched her work on this one step, which the great choreographer did so easily and which she struggled so hard to emulate. I never saw anyone work so hard, sweat streaming down her face, her shirt wet and sticking to her body. Over and over: tap one, two, three with the right foot, pirouette, tap one, two, three with the left foot, then tap-tap, bounce, tap-tap, swanee to the right, tap-tap, bounce, swanee to the left, then a shuffle-off-to-Buffalo exit to the right. When Marilyn bounced, *everything* bounced. She was electric—I couldn't take my eyes off her.

"Gettin' there, kid," Cole kept encouraging her. "Again! And a six, seven, eight ... " And they would do it again, both staring at the big mirror, Cole watching her, Marilyn's gaze glued to herself.

After a while, I got a little bored just watching, so I took out a sketch pad from my briefcase and began sketching. How did Marilyn look? First of all, if Jacobs hadn't told me, I would never have known who it was. She had no lipstick or eye makeup, her straggly hair was partially contained by a cloth band, her face was covered with freckles, and the gray under her eyes made her look as though she'd stayed up too late every night since puberty. But her body, not insulted by a shred of underwear beneath the T-shirt and shorts, still looked great.

At the break, Marilyn came over, sweaty and panting, to see what I was doing. I'd just started, but she said in that oft-imitated but inimitable breathy whisper, "Well, we're quite the artist, aren't we."

Then she went back to work.

As I watched and drew, I thought of the story Jacobs had told me about Marilyn and Robert Mitchum. On the set of *River of No Return*, Mitchum had seen her reading a dictionary of Freudian terms. "I'm starting the chapter called 'anal eroticism,'" she announced. Then she asked shyly: "Robert, what exactly is eroticism?" Mitchum

explained. A minute later, she looked up from the book again and asked, "Robert, what is anal?"

And then there was the story about her and Don Murray on the set of *Bus Stop.* "Don, do you know what a phallic symbol is?" Don was supposed to have replied, "Know what it is? I've *got one!*"

It occurred to me to ask Miss Monroe if these stories were apocryphal, but then I thought it best not to. When

Jacobs finally arrived to pick me up, Marilyn came over to look at the sketch I was just finishing, the one reproduced on page 45.

"Oh my," she gasped. "Do I look that bad? I'll pay you zillions not to show it to anyone!"

I assured her I wouldn't let anyone see it. And I haven't until now. My second portrait here, which was reproduced by the hundreds, was done from photos and, as you can see, is less Norma Jean Baker and more the Marilyn Monroe that the world has loved these many years.

This was the era when everyone in the studios was complaining about Marilyn's absences and tardiness, but all I saw in that brief time with her was talent, humility, and dedication.

I like the recent quote of director Billy Wilder's on Marilyn's legendary tardiness, which says it all: "On the other hand, I have an Aunt Ida in Vienna who is always on time, but I wouldn't put her in a movie."

During the second session of posing for his portrait, Robert Mitchum came over and studied it, one eyebrow cocked critically.

"You sure made me look like a mean sonofabitch," he said.

"I didn't, Robert," I replied, pointing skyward. "God did."

Mitchum isn't really mean. He's one of the most humorous—and intelligent—men I know. He is a great storyteller, telling fantastic tales complete with a variety of different voices and accents only he can do. One evening at a small dinner party, I watched him hold his own on the subject of global politics with none other than the redoubtable and intimidating Clare Booth Luce.

I first met him when he came into El Matador in 1955. He stayed all evening, and somewhere along the line he wrote this in our guest book:

Compadre—
    When all the broken crockery of desperate communion is swept from under our understanding heels we may find on that clear expanse of floor the true and irrevocable target of infinite thrust.

I am still working on deciphering it.

Clearer was his reaction to interviewers during a 1985 nationally televised tribute to the Betty Ford Center.

Mitchum joined Liza Minnelli, Elizabeth Taylor, and others to honor Mrs. Ford and the center she had created for combating alcoholism. Mitchum had recently "graduated" from the center and had come to express his admiration for the program.

"Now let me get this straight," said the master of ceremonies, "you no longer drink any alcohol whatsoever?"

"Well, I didn't exactly say that," drawled Mitchum to the world. "I just don't fall on my ass anymore."

Then a reporter asked Mitchum, "Didn't you learn anything in your thirty days there at the Betty Ford Center?"

"Oh, sure!" replied the unflappable Mitchum. "I learned to put more ice in my drinks."

The camera mercifully didn't register Mrs. Ford's reaction.

Married for more than half a century to the same fine woman, Bob's take on marriage is priceless. When asked the secret of his fidelity in light of Hollywood's traditional marital restlessness and today's permissiveness, Mitchum replied, "Lack of imagination, I guess."

Walking down the street with America's favorite crooner was a major event, as I found out one fall day. After lunch at El Matador (we served a smorgasbord at noon for a few experimental months), Bing Crosby and I started down Montgomery Street to a sporting goods store. As we came out of my saloon, the singer was spotted by the first of a series of people.

"H'ya Bing!" an elderly man sang out, his face lit up at recognizing The Great Man and his hand stabbed out for a shake.

"How ya' doin'!" Bing responded. He didn't take his hands out of his raincoat, and he didn't slow his walk, but there was genuine friendliness in that deep voice, perhaps the most famous voice of his time, a sunshiny, folksy, neighborly, melodic voice.

"Remember me?" said the man, walking along with us, keeping up with Bing's steady pace. "Elmer Sommers? 'Bout ten years ago?"

"Sure!" said Bing. "You still down there?"

"Naw," said the man. "I left there thirteen years ago! Over in Alameda now."

"Great!" said Bing.

"What a memory!" said the man. "Didn't think you'd remember me."

"Keep up the good work, Elmer!" Bing said as we moved away down the street.

"Where'd you know him?" I asked.

"Never saw him before," said Bing with a chuckle.

"But—"

"Great utilitarian phrase, that," he explained. "'Still down there?' Works for everyone. Everyone's 'down there' somewhere. They either are or they aren't still down there."

A pretty blonde girl accosted him next as we made our way down the sidewalk. "Bing!" she gasped, her face flushed with excitement. "Bet you don't remember me!"

"Sure I do," Bing said without stopping.

"Carol! I'm Carol."

"I knew that," said Bing. "It was your last name I . . . "

"Osloman," she finished.

"Of course, Carol. You still down there?"

"Yep. Still at good old Universal Travel! Remember when you came in—about five years ago and you gave me an autograph for my son?"

"Course," said Bing. "Say hello to him!"

This parade of people continued all the way to the store. I marveled at Bing's adroit handling of each and every one, from all walks of life. They all acted as though they knew him well, as though they owned part of him.

"How do you do it?" I asked.

"Trick is to keep moving," Bing said. "Once you stop, you're dead. The other thing is, try not to shake hands. They'll grab you and hang on, and there you are, draggin' 'em down the sidewalk to get where you're going. You keep your hands in your pockets."

"How do you stand it?"

Bing shrugged. "They're all nice. They're all well-wishers."

Strangely enough, when we went to the prize fights, which we did often, people—the special fraternity of prize fight aficionados—seemed inclined to leave him alone, except to ask him which boxer he was betting on. He liked it this way. In spite of the air of friendliness and easy, good-old-boyness that was his stock in trade, Bing was very much a loner. All the world was his friend, but he had very few real friends. He liked to tell stories about Bob Hope and Dorothy Lamour and others, but his only close friend in show biz was the bandleader and comedian Phil Harris.

"People don't believe it," Phil told me recently. "But Bing was shy with most people. That's why he drank."

Drank? Shy?

"I never saw him drink too much," I said. "I heard his first wife had a problem, but . . . "

"Hell, people say I drink! Bing was drinking a quart a day there! That was only until he married Kathy. Then he mostly quit." (I found out recently that Bing was jailed for a month in 1930 for a vehicular death when he was driving, and in 1953 he had another drunken driving "incident" where a woman was injured.)

A favorite star of Bing's stories, one of his few good friends, was the late Joe Frisco, the stuttering comic who was an habitué of the racetracks.

"Went to Santa Anita once," Bing drawled. "There was Joe at the gate all excited. 'B-B-Bing, I got a h-h-hot one in the third! Long, long s-s-shot, but I got it from the j-j-jockey himself. B-B-Bing, he's fixed to win! Lend me a tw-tw-twenty.'" Bing chuckled at the memory. "By gosh, if that horse didn't come in at forty to one! Afterward, I go up to the club house and Joe's already there ensconced at a table, a big cigar jutting out of his mouth, a jeroboam of the bubbly at his elbow, and his arms around two good-lookin' bimbos. When he spots me, he casually takes out his wad of bills, peels off a twenty, and says, 'Here ya' go, b-boy-boy, give us a chorus of "M-m-melancholy B-b-baby"!'" Bing laughed. "Man, I sure miss Joe."

"Did you give him his chorus?" I asked.

"Two!" he said and shook his head. "Sure miss Joe."

People assumed he and Bob Hope were constant companions, but the truth is they seldom saw each other.

"Bob's whole life is show business. That's all he talks or thinks about. A little of that goes a long way with me. Too many other important things in life."

I met Bing for the first time in 1960. I had received a call in my San Francisco studio from his very English butler, Fisher, who was previously employed by the Royal Family. He was one of the great characters of all time, straight out of Wodehouse. "Mistuh Crawsby has seen your *pawtraits* in El Matador and is interested in having *pawtraits* done of his children. Could you come around 'the scatter,' as he calls it, to discuss the matter? Hah-hah, sir, matter, scatter, there's a bit of a rhyme!"

The next day I drove down to the "scatter," a mansion in a posh suburb south of San Francisco; I knew my way around the Carolands, having grown up in Hillsborough. I parked in the driveway, and as I approached the imposing front door, I heard a familiar, a very familiar, the most familiar, voice singing "King of the Road." If I'd been at the door of any other house, I would have assumed that someone was playing the radio.

Bing himself opened the door. "Hey, how are ya'!" he said. "Heard this new song 'King of the Road'? Great song."

Shorter than I imagined, bald without his toupee, with a leathery tan, great smile, warm voice, and cold blue eyes—here was the man who'd made seventy feature films and sold over 500 million records in his long career.

That day we began a group portrait of his three young children, Harry, Nathaniel, and Mary Frances. As I worked,

Fisher would hover about, Jeeves-like, making lofty criti-
cisms designed to help the project along. ("A little something wrong with Master Harry's mouth, sir, if I may say
so.") Over the next three months, I finished the children's
portrait, did a life-size oil painting of Bing and his dog, a
large pastel of his wife, Katherine, plus the charcoal study
reproduced on page 50.

"Do me in a hat," said Bing, "so I don't have to wear
that rug."

Bing was a fine model, posing with his beloved labra-
dor and his favorite Purdy shotgun, not moving and yet
singing the entire time. I realized early on that this man
didn't just sing for a living—he truly *loved* to sing. Once
we went duck shooting on his ranch in Northern California, and when we were out in the blinds on a freezing October dawn, I heard that great voice wafting down the
marshes in an improvisation beginning, "Where are you,
Ducky Darlin', now that I want you so bad . . . "

I've heard stories about Bing's supposed coldness, of
how he could "disappear" people around him when he
was displeased, but I never saw that side. I think Bing and
I became friends because he knew I wanted nothing from
him. Also, sports were his life: a one-time scratch golfer,
he was passionately involved in all sports, and he knew I
was available at the drop of a hat to go to the Golden
Gloves or to a game. He liked going to the fights because
"no one's going to take my picture, so I don't have to wear
that damned rug." He hated his toupee with a passion.
There was little pretense about Bing.

He was a fine fly fisherman and took it very seriously.
I wish I had a picture of him the time we went for big
trout in a gin-clear spring creek in Northern California.
"These big guys spook easily. They feel the vibrations of
our feet on the bank and stop feeding," he said as we approached the stream. So there the two of us were, sneak-

ing across the tundra on all fours, and Bing whispered back over his shoulder to me, "As we say in Alaska, if you're not the lead sled dog, the view never changes."

I'm a fair fisherman, but I caught none that day. Bing's lovely delicate casts brought in three large trout. He released them tenderly, massaging them in the water first so that they might live to fight another day.

I remember on that trip I asked Bing, one of the great entertainers, who he thought was the best.

"Greatest I ever saw was Al Jolson," said Bing. "Maybe doesn't sound it on records—you had to see him in person—but he was mesmerizing. Second was Maurice Chevalier. Guy could walk out on a stage, not much of a voice, just that enormous charm, and hold you in the palm of his hand for two hours."

Bing loved to write letters, even when a phone call would have been easier. I have a stack of them. He loved words like "bibulous" and "litigious" and "discombobulated" and "preprandial" as well as alliteration for its own sake. ("That was both a languorous and lively literary luncheon that your lovely lady laid out for us . . . ")

He had enormous clout in the entertainment industry, but he wielded it gracefully and seldom. One day I mentioned that the San Francisco Film Festival, whose board I was on, wanted to honor Walt Disney with a retrospective but had encountered resistance about Disney actually coming to San Francisco in person.

"Let me give it a try," said Bing. "I did the narration for free for Walt's *Headless Horseman,* so he owes me one."

He reached for the phone, got right through to Disney, and the brief, productive conversation ended: "So Walt, that's great, you'll bring a print of *Snow White* with you, and my friend Barny Conrad will pick you up at the airport on the seventeenth. And Walt, thanks a lot."

What Bing wanted, Bing usually got.

One afternoon I came home from my studio, and my wife said, "Call Bing Crosby. He wants to go to the fights tonight."

Our six-year-old daughter, Kendall, said, mouth agape, "You're going to call *Bing Crosby?!* Can I listen on the other phone?"

"You certainly may not," I said. "You don't even know who Bing Crosby is."

"Yes, I do," she countered. "I do!"

"All right, then," I challenged as I dialed. "*Who* is Bing Crosby?"

"He is," she said solemnly, standing up and saluting, "the President of the United States of America!"

I told Bing when he answered, and he chuckled appreciatively. "I'll settle for that, Barn," he said. "Let me talk to her."

He was great with my kids and with his own three, driving them to school every day (in the Rolls) and planning all sorts of activities and trips with them.

"We parents do too much *for* our kids and not enough *with* them," he said to me once. "I messed up with my first batch, the four boys, did everything wrong. Not going to do it this time." Another time he said, "I've learned the hard way that kids need affection the most when they deserve it the least." He puffed on his unlit pipe and added, "Adults, too."

Bing's older son, Harry, by Katherine, was with his father when I last saw Bing, shortly before his death, and I have never encountered a closer father and son relationship. Mary and I had been invited down to Bing's ramshackle house at Las Cruces in Baja California, for a few days. He seemed so much happier there, "away from the social ramble," in the happy disarray of this home rather than in his over-decorated Hillsborough mansion, with its cabinets of Fabergé eggs and equestrian paintings by Herrick. Bing, seventy-four years old, was frail and shaky due to a terrible twenty-foot fall from a Pasadena stage a year before.

"The orchestra had been taken down to the basement on their platform during the last number," he said, rubbing his ribcage. "Then it was supposed to come right back up for me to turn around, step onto it, and say goodnight to the audience. Someone goofed and it wasn't sent back up. I turned and stepped out onto straight air! As I was falling, kind of swimming desperately, I caught on to some trellis decoration that slowed down my fall, or I would have been killed. Fell flat on my back. It's been a little rough coming back from that."

But against his doctor's vehement orders, he was planning a two-week engagement at the London Palladium. The show involved appearances by his three youngest children, all of whom are highly talented musically.

"I guess I shouldn't do it," said Bing, who was still on a cane. "The doctors are mad at me, very upset. But the kids are really counting on it. Gotta do it. It will give them a boost into the business that they want so badly."

Before we left, Bing autographed a photo to our daughter, now a successful model: "To Kendall—with love from the President of the United States."

Bing went to England, did the exhausting show to enormous acclaim, and even added a special performance for the Queen. It was a gallant effort and a true triumph of will and spirit, but it left him exhausted. When it was over, he went to Spain to rest.

The second day in Madrid, October 14, 1977, Bing played in a tournament with his idol, Seve Ballesteros, and they won. As they were walking triumphantly off the eighteenth tee, Bing faltered, stumbled, and fell dead.

It was reported that he was singing when the heart attack struck. Of course he was. And you know what? He still is. Try to get through Christmas without hearing his poignant "White Christmas" a dozen times or more.

Every July, Bing's old friend Phil Harris, the great band-leader and entertainer, used to stop off at El Matador on his way to "the Grove." (This is the nickname for the yearly gathering that the Bohemian Club of San Francisco hosts in a redwood grove near Santa Rosa.) One of the highlights of the year at the Mat was listening to Phil Harris, one of the last of the great raconteurs, tell his stories, many of which were about his beloved wife of many decades, actress Alice Faye.

"Y'know, it was Alice's and my big anniversary last month, and so I really did it right. I took that gorgeous woman to the same little restaurant in the valley that I used to take her to when we was courtin', and I had candles on the table, y'know, and a special wine, y'know, and let me tell you it was romantic as hell. Then we went to this fancy motel and went to bed, and let me tell you it started out just great, and let me tell you I was the old Phil Harris, comin' on strong and virile, and y'know what, just then that damned earthquake struck and threw me out of bed. And it woke Alice up.

"And y'know, it's not true that I'm too old for sex. Why, Alice and me, we still play around plenty with our little sexy games. One I especially like is where Alice grabs it at the base and I grab it at the top, and then we both count to three, let go, and bet which way it's going to fall."

He told of an incident that happened in Madison Square Garden years back. Gladys Gooding was a redoubtable, stout, and proper soprano who traditionally sang the "Star-Spangled Banner" before important athletic events. On this particular night at a prize fight, the calliope-voiced announcer boomed out over the public address system: "And now, Miss Gladys Gooding will sing our national anthem!"

At that point a voice from the bleachers shouted down, "Gladys Gooding sucks!"

The announcer looked stunned but only hesitated a moment. "Nevertheless," he said, continuing coolly, "she will now sing the 'Star-Spangled Banner.'"

Born in 1904, it is amazing to see Phil sing and perform on stage with the vigor of a man half his age. When someone commented on his energy recently, he took another sip of bourbon and shook his head apologetically.

"Yeah, I know it," he said in that inimitable raspy voice, "I am an affront to clean living. But I get it from my grandmother. She was a very strong woman. She buried three husbands—and two of 'em were only napping."

D riving down Broadway near the Matador one morning, I was surprised to see that denizen of Beverly Hills, actor Ricardo Montalban. (He who was unfailingly called "Ricky Mendelbaum" by Sam Goldwyn.)

Ricardo was walking down the sidewalk, arm in arm with comely actress Elizabeth Ashley. I hadn't seen him for a couple of years and wondered what brought him to the city. I slowed down my car and drove alongside the couple while they strolled along.

"Hey, Ricardo," I called out my window. "*Qué haces por aquí?* What are you doing here?"

He kept walking, unsmiling, not looking at me, saying out of the corner of his mouth, "I am working, Bernabé!"

Forty-five years living in this country and he still hasn't lost a bit of his accent.

"Great!" I said. "How long are you going to be in town? Come into the Matador and I'll buy you a drink."

"I'm working!" he said vehemently and, I thought, rather rudely. "*Trabajando!* Keep going!"

I still didn't get it. Then I heard an angry voice yell, "Cut!" I looked up to see a camera crew on the roof of a building and the director on the roof of another.

I had just ruined a very expensive shot in Ricardo's latest film, and it cost me several rounds of drinks later in the Matador for the entire crew.

"I'm going to be a writer if it kills me!" said one of the first customers in my saloon. He wasn't a star then. Unknown and unpublished, Alex Haley was destined to be a writer who would command the attention of the world.

I had first met Alex in 1951 when I was teaching creative writing in an adult education program at the Marina High School in San Francisco. He was a cook in the Coast Guard and had achieved considerable success in a strange branch of writing: while at sea, he would write imaginative love letters at a dollar a pop for his ship-mates, who would subsequently reap fine rewards on shore from the objects of their affections. He was a steady customer at El Matador. He didn't drink, but he hung around the bar, always hoping to meet people in the writing game who could help him achieve his lifelong ambition of being a writer. He had little natural talent, but he was a good storyteller, worked hard at writing every day, read everything about writing, and never gave up. He finally sold a little piece about the Coast Guard to the Sunday newspaper supplement "This Week." He said, "They paid me one hundred dollars. I went and got it cashed into one hundred one-dollar bills. I had fifty in one pocket and fifty in the other, and I walked down the street squeezing them—oh, that tactile feeling." In the Matador that night, we broke out a bottle of champagne to celebrate.

One night the author Budd Schulberg flew in from New York and came to the Matador; I phoned Alex in Oakland, and he sped over the bridge to San Francisco in record time. Alex's favorite books happened to be *Waterfront* and *What Makes Sammy Run,* and he was thrilled to meet the

author of them. They sat in the bar and talked till four in the morning. Budd encouraged Alex's writing, and in a few months *Reader's Digest* published "My Most Unforgettable Character," an essay by Alex on his Pullman porter father. His career, while not exactly soaring, was beginning to take off. He did countless articles for many different magazines such as *True, Argosy,* and *True Confessions.* He always said the confession magazines were a great training ground for learning the importance of conflict and characterization. Then he had a great breakthrough: he created a question and answer format while writing an article on trumpeter Miles Davis, and this became the style for the so-called *Playboy* interview. Alex had been given six weeks to write six thousand words. Halfway through he realized he didn't have enough to write the article.

"Miles was monosyllabic," he said. "If you're a friend of Miles Davis, around 6:30 in the afternoon the phone might ring and a voice would come on and say, 'Chili,' and hang up. The translation was that he had cooked up a mess of chili, and you should come over and partake.

"So what I did, because I was desperate to get into that magazine, I took a gamble. I took half of that six thousand words and did the best I could—rewrote and rewrote—an essay about his world. Then I took the other three thousand words, took every utterance he'd made, and made up questions to make it seem he'd answered them. I took it to the editors and the readers liked the style."

That style for the *Playboy* interview still exists today.

He did many such interviews for that magazine, including one with the infamous neo-Nazi and racist George Lincoln Rockwell. Alex's bizarre encounter with the self-styled führer occurred at his extensive headquarters in Arlington, Virginia. When *Playboy* called Rockwell to set up the interview, the neo-Nazi agreed "as long as you don't send down one of your Jews."

When Alex called to tell Rockwell when he was arriving, the man said, "Now, you're sure you're not a Jew?"

"Uh, no," Alex assured him. "No, uh, I am *definitely* not a Jew."

"Okay then," said Rockwell. "I'll give you one hour."

Once he arrived, Alex was escorted by burly, uniformed men past Nazi flags and portraits of Hitler to Rockwell's office. "Sieg heil!" the guards said, as they opened the door. Rockwell's jaw dropped when he saw that Alex was black.

"Jesus Christ," he said. Still, he reluctantly agreed to go ahead with the interview.

"But let's get this one thing straight!" growled Rockwell, leaning back in his chair. "I regard you and your people as no better than chimpanzees."

"That's fine," said the unflappable Haley. "You're welcome to your opinion." As they started the interview, Alex spotted an electric typewriter on a stand by the desk.

"Mr. Rockwell, I generally take notes on a typewriter. May I use that one?"

Rockwell looked at him and exclaimed pointedly, "But it's electric!"

Alex smiled back. "I think I can manage, sir."

Alex began the questioning and typed the answers as Rockwell gave them with exaggerated slowness.

"Sir, you may speak faster," said Alex, who once won a championship speed-typing contest in California.

"Well, when I was born . . . "

"You may talk faster, sir."

Rockwell went a little faster, at normal speed, and Alex recorded the words almost as they were spoken. Rockwell speeded up, and Alex kept up with him. Faster and faster Rockwell spoke, and Alex's typing went right along with him. Rockwell stopped and gazed at Haley in unfeigned amazement. Alex looked back, shrugged, and said modestly, à la Stepin Fetchit, "Pretty good for a chimpanzee, eh man?"

Later, Alex wrote the successful biography of Malcolm X, which has sold over six million copies. But he had an even bigger book inside of him, begging to get out: the story of his origins, his roots, told in the form of his own family's oral history, which had been passed down to him by his grandmother and aunts on the front porch of their house in Henning, Tennessee—a story that could be that of virtually every black American. At first he called it *Before This Anger*, and he wrote part of it in my studio while I was living in Tahiti. Upon my return, I was so moved as he told me the story that, even before he had finished writing it, I sent him to Hollywood to see my agent, lawyer Louis Blau. Blau is highly successful, tough, and always frantically busy with clients, who include many famous stars, directors, and writers.

"I'll give you fifteen minutes to tell your story, Mr. Haley," he said. "That's all the time I have."

Alex began to recount in his quiet way the saga of Kunta Kinte, his ancestor, who was captured in the rain forest of the upper Gambia River in Africa. Kinte was brought in chains to America and sold to Dr. William Waller of Spotsylvania County, Virginia. Alex began to tell the story of Chicken George, of Tizzy, and of the entire larger-than-life family—the great tapestry of characters that would eventually be known throughout the world of literature and television as *Roots.*

At the end of fifteen minutes, Blau told his secretary to cancel all his appointments and telephone calls and sat riveted for two hours as Alex told the entire tumultuous story of all the generations that had preceded his birth. Blau said not a word until Alex had finished with the last sentence: "And that little baby was me."

Then Blau stood up slowly, extended his hand, and said huskily, "Mr. Haley, if you can write that story the way you just told it, you will change the world!"

Alex could and Alex did.

And before that day with Blau ended, Alex had a deal to make the TV series that more people in the world would see than any other in history.

After *Roots* became a runaway bestseller and won both the Pulitzer Prize and a National Book Award, Alex Haley was in great demand as a speaker. He gave one talk at Simpson College in the little town of Indianola, Iowa, to a crowd of one thousand people, and afterward, autographing books, he noticed one man, a patrician-looking person, who seemed to want to speak to him but was hanging back diffidently. Alex finally said, "Sir, did you wish to say something to me?"

The man cleared his throat and said, "Mr. Haley, I'm the academic dean here, and I read your book, and I checked my family records. I'm a genealogy buff like you."

"Yes?" said Alex.

"Well, I'm not sure how to put this delicately."

"Yes, go on."

"Well, it would appear, Mr. Haley, that Dr. William Waller, my great-great-great-great-grandfather owned your great-great-great-great-grandfather, Kunta Kinte."

Alex told me later, "There we stood, staring at each other, the mutually great-great-great-great-grandsons of the late-1760s master and slave. In Dr. Waller Wiser's home, we exchanged lineages into the wee hours and became friends for life."

Not all of Alex's stories about his family are in *Roots*. He told me one about his father, which directly shaped Alex's and his siblings' lives.

Simon Haley, the son of a former slave and sharecropper from Savannah, Tennessee, was determined not to end his days as a field hand. He worked his way through high school and struggled partially through A & T College in Greensboro, North Carolina. However, he began to feel he'd have to give up his dream of an education because of the double burden of earning both his living and the tuition fee. He took a job as a Pullman porter while deciding whether or not to return home to sharecropping. On one of his trips, he waited on R. S. M. Boyce, a retired executive of the Curtis Publishing Company, who took an interest in the polite, alert young man. Boyce asked him about his life and his ambitions. Later, he sent Simon five hundred dollars, enough for full living expenses and tuition for a year at college. This enabled Simon to graduate, first in his class, and win a scholarship to Cornell University for his master's.

Thus Alex, instead of growing up on a farm in bleak sharecropping poverty, was reared in an atmosphere of books and the love of learning, and he became a writer; his brother George is chairman of the U.S. Postal Rate Commission; his brother Julius is an architect; and his sister, Lois, is a music teacher. All because of one man's generosity on a train way back in 1918.

Alex was always the storyteller; one he told us in El Matador reflected the kind of simple man of great values that he was. He described a cousin from his hometown, an arrogant and conceited young man who flaunted his education. He never left home without his Phi Beta Kappa key dangling from a gold chain around his neck. One day, an elderly aunt took a close look at the cousin's Phi Beta key, wrinkled her old brow, and said: "Ver' nice, boy, ver' nice, but what do it *open?*"

Alex is gone now, and I will simply say, in the words of George Bernard Shaw, "I can lose a friend like that by *my* death but not by his."

"Hey, where were you last night?" Herb Caen asked on the phone reproachfully. "We brought Truman Capote into the Matador."

I was disappointed, since I'd always admired the man's writing. "Bring him to lunch at home tomorrow," I said.

I'd heard Truman was petite, but the next day, when I opened the front door of our Belvedere house, for a moment I thought he was one of the neighborhood kids. Then I looked down. He had on his mushroom panama hat with the brim turned down all around and the trademark long scarf flung around his neck, even though it was a sunny California afternoon.

"Hi," he said in that childlike girlish twang. "I'm Tru, and you're Barney Google."

He stepped into our living room, followed by Herb Caen and his girlfriend. Before Truman could sit down, a black-and-white shape burst out of the bedroom and headed straight for him.

Debbie Dog, an inbred Boston bull terrier, was a menace, and I'd begged my then-wife, Dale, to kindly lock her in the bathroom for the duration of our famous visitor's stay. Debbie Dog was a congenital biter. She had bitten the postman, the meter reader, every delivery boy, my mother, and every friend we'd ever had. The vet would only handle her with thick gloves. She bit me regularly, deeply, and delightedly, twice attacking me from behind when I was taking an unguarded pee. Only Dale could handle her.

Now she'd escaped and was streaking toward our illustrious guest. I envisioned the juicy lawsuit.

"That dog bites!" I shouted in warning. But before any fangs could sink into those stumpy legs, I saw an amazing thing: Truman bent over, scooped the charging creature up, and cradled her in his arms like a newborn baby.

"Bulldog!" he cooed to it. "Bulldog!"

Debbie Dog went limp, and her eyes closed happily as Truman rocked her back and forth.

"They like to be told who they are," said Truman, sitting in a chair. "I've had a dozen of 'em, my favorite animal. Bulldog, bulldog!"

I made drinks, and Truman talked for two hours, gossiping shamelessly and telling wonderfully bizarre stories, while constantly reassuring the dog in his arms.

"You've heard about what happened to Buffy Vanderpool, didn't you? You know her, of course. Buffy? Buffy Vanderpool of Sag Harbor? You *must* know her! *Everyone* knows Buffy." We looked blank and he shrugged his dismay at our provincial unawareness. "Anyway, six months ago—bulldog! bulldog!—Buffy and her son, Taylor, were roughing it on this remote Greek island in the

Aegean, sleeping in sleeping bags on the beach. One midnight they were awakened by this terrible sound, the sound of little feet, and in the moonlight—bulldog, bulldog—they saw pouring out of the ruins of this old temple on the hill hundreds of huge rats, creatures almost as big as this bulldog, and they swarmed down to the beach and attacked Buffy and her son in their sleeping bags. And she cried, 'Run, Taylor, run into the water!' and they leapt out of their sleeping bags and rushed into the water, but one of the rats bit off the end of Buffy's nose, and a great horde of them pulled Taylor down into the waves and he drowned. But Buffy got away from them and kept swimming and swimming, and she was picked up half dead at six in the morning by a Greek trawler—bulldog, bulldog—and she's still at Mayo's for therapy and plastic surgery. But she's doing *much* better."

Many other stories followed that afternoon, all slightly bizarre but somehow believable when Truman told them. And Debbie Dog never left his arms. Our house was on the water, and when a seagull lit on the dock, Truman gave a stagey little shudder.

"Awful birds!" he said. Then suddenly confidential, "They can be *very* dangerous, you know. There's a place in Maine where they are especially vicious—bulldog, bulldog. I go to visit this friend of mine, an old woman named Alma, Alma Wilson Smith—Bingham?—and she used to like to go down to the point and feed these terrible seagulls, but she'd always take a big umbrella because these damn birds are so predatory. She'd fling out the food, then quickly open the umbrella as protection as these birds would—*screak, screak*—descend around her in a frenzy. Last year she was doing that, and you know what, it was awful, just *awful!* She flung out the food, and the umbrella stuck and wouldn't open—*screak, screak*—and those damned creatures attacked her and pecked out both her eyes—bulldog, bulldog."

Truman was in the Bay Area to participate in a study of creativity conducted by the University of California at Berkeley. It lasted two weeks, and I saw him several times in the Matador with Herb Caen. One day he told us of an interesting experiment that the university had done with him and four other well-known authors. They were each put in a cubicle where they could not see their fellow authors, but they could see a screen that displayed the responses made by the others to a quiz. Anonymous to each other during the test, they were designated on the screen by a letter of the alphabet. Truman was the last, with "E."

He said, "The first question was: Who was the greatest astronomer: Galileo, Copernicus, Newton, or Hipparchus?

I was going to put down Galileo, but I looked up at the screen and saw that 'A' had put Hipparchus and 'B' had put Hipparchus and 'C' had put Hipparchus and 'D' had put Hipparchus. So shit, what the hell, I'd never heard of the gentleman, but if these smart guys all thought Hipparchus was the tops, I'd put him down, too."

Then came music. "Generally considered to be the greatest musician is: Beethoven, Bach, Mozart, or Strindberg. Well, I was going to put Beethoven, but 'A' put Strindberg, 'B' put Strindberg, 'C' put Strindberg, 'D' put Strindberg, and so I figured they knew a lot that I didn't about Mister Strindberg, so I put down Strindberg."

Then came mathematics. "Now there's a subject I know diddly-squat about, so when the Big Boys all picked someone named Schwartz over Einstein and Pythagoras, I tagged right along with Schwartz. And so it went, until we got to this question: The greatest writer is: Tolstoy, Cervantes, George Bernard Shaw, or Gogol. And 'A' put Gogol, 'B' put Gogol, 'C' put Gogol, and 'D' put Gogol! I said, *Gogol!!* Now wait just a damn minute here! I said to hell with the others, and I put down Tolstoy."

Truman chuckled. "At the end of the day, we found out to our chagrin that each one of us had been told that we were 'E'! We each thought we were the last. It was a test to find out how influenced we were by our peers' opinions. We all did lousily, I was happy to learn, and me the worst."

Truman was very fond of Herb Caen, whom he called Monkey-head when he didn't call him Herbaceous. "Listen, Monkey-head, I *really* like your new girl friend—she's so wonderfully *neurotic!*"

One day, Herb and Truman and I were having lunch after I had done a charcoal sketch of Truman (which is now in the National Portrait Gallery of the Smithsonian; see page 68), and Truman pulled out a letter.

"It's from Brando," he said. "Seven pages of bile and vitriol and vilification."

Truman had written a touching but devastating profile of the actor, which had appeared in *The New Yorker* magazine. He had been sent to Tokyo, where Marlon was making the film *Sayonara;* they'd sat up all night drinking in his hotel room, and the usually reticent actor had poured out his heart to Truman. Truman had used his old interviewing trick of first telling intimate details of his own childhood, putting the quarry off-guard, and then encouraging him to reveal his own secrets. It had worked. Among other things Marlon had told of his wretched childhood, of how he used to come home from school to find his mother passed out from drink, how he'd have to put her to bed, and the terrible shame of it all. Truman showed me Marlon's letter in which he expressed his anger, his hurt, and his feeling of betrayal over the article.

"I trusted you. I told you things that night I've never told another living soul. How could you have *done* this to me?!"

"Well, golly gee," Truman sniffed, as he put the letter back in his pocket, "I've written him back, and I said, 'Listen here, Mister Marlon Brando, I *told* you right off the bat when I arrived in Japan that I was working for *The New Yorker.* In what capacity did you think I was working for them?' He giggled. 'Selling advertising space in the magazine?'"

A couple of years later he was back in San Francisco, this time traveling with one of the principal characters in his nonfiction book *In Cold Blood*—the detective in the famous murder case, with whom Truman had remained a great friend. Truman was fascinated with criminals at the time and had visited hundreds of prisoners and dozens of death-row inmates, including several in Charles Manson's gang.

"Everyone in prison says he isn't guilty," he said at lunch. "But you know what?" He whispered, "They're *all* guilty." Then he giggled. "I always want so bad to believe they've been framed, but you find out they're *all* lying."

"You know something weird? Of the five people killed by the Manson gang, I had met four—each independently of the others. Think of the odds against *that!* And speaking of strange coincidences, how about this: I knew both Bobby Kennedy and J.F.K., and I knew both their killers! How about that! Met Lee Oswald in Moscow just after he defected, and met Sirhan Saran-wrap, as I call him, in prison."

As for the portrait I did, I don't think he liked it. All he said was, "Oh my, oh me oh my!"

Truman wanted to go hunting for his passion—fancy paper weights. So I took him up and down Union Street. People stared at him wherever he went whether they knew who he was or not; he *did* look different. He spent several hundred dollars on one paper weight that afternoon and was very happy. At one point, while shopping, he asked me what I was working on.

"A novel called *Dangerfield*," I said.

"Gorgeous title!" he said. "And why is the field dangerous?"

"It's one word," I said. "It's the man's name."

"Oh no, no, no, no!" he said. "It must be two words! *Danger Field!*"

"But it's the main character's name," I protested.

"Change it," Truman said. "Rename him Smedrood and call the book *Danger Field!*"

For better or worse, I didn't take his advice.

Later he said, "I'm thinking of writing something called *A Massive Insult to the Brain*. That's what they call it in the hospital when you die of too much alcohol. Isn't that just a *delicious* title?"

I suppose few people have ever been as self-destructive as Truman. Toward the end, I remember seeing him on a Los Angeles talk show so drugged and/or drunk he could hardly stay upright in the chair. But he could still tell stories.

"People are so funny," he slurred. "I was in this restaurant the other night, and this woman, she'd had a few, came over, and she was wearing this bare midriff outfit, and she stands in front of me, and says, 'You're famous. Sign my stomach.' And she hands me a felt pen. So I laughed and signed her tummy. She went back to the table, and I could see that she and her husband were having a tiff, a real mister-and-missus, and then *he* gets up and lurches over, and says belligerently, 'Well, Mister Famous Author, as long as you're signing things, how about signing this.' And right then and there he unzips his fly and whips it out. And I said, 'Well, sir, I might be able to *initial* that, but I'd never be able to autograph it.' That kind of took care of *him!*"

Quite unnecessarily, the interviewer, on the air, decided to ask sternly, "Mr. Capote, sir, have you been drinking?"

"You mean"—long, long pause—"*immediate* drinking?"

Not many weeks afterward he suffered that massive insult to the brain. At Truman's funeral, someone asked Artie Shaw what Truman had died of.

"He died," replied the musician sorrowfully, "of living." Then Artie brightened at a memory. "Once I asked Louis Armstrong—never Louie—what a mutual friend had died of. 'Man,' said Louis, 'when you die, you die of *everything!*'"

Truman died of everything. His one great love in life was writing, it was his *everything,* and he felt he'd lost that. Perhaps as good an epitaph as any for him is this passage from *Other Voices, Other Rooms:* "We work in the dark, we do what we can, we give what we have. Our doubt is our passion, and our passion is our task."

Part Two

sk anyone in Hollywood, New York, or London theatrical circles: David Niven had no equal in storytelling. He certainly was the finest who ever graced the portals of El Matador. Amusing as his book of memoirs, *The Moon Is a Balloon,* is, it still cannot catch the flavor, the sly suavity, the delightful raunchiness that he imparted when he told his stories in person. They were never jokes as such—they were incidents, highly embellished, small adventures that happened to him and his pals during his amazing career as an army officer and movie star.

He told my wife and me the following story in 1962, over drinks at El Matador, and somehow, the way David told it, it wasn't particularly shocking.

"My darling wife and I had a bit of a tiff and had separated for a couple of months, but then, to my great joy, we agreed to get back together. She was flying in from Sweden, and I was to meet her that night at the Burbank Airport at nine. I was very excited. My wife, Hjordis, is one of the most beautiful girls in the world." (He pronounced the word *girls* somewhat the way Maurice Chevalier did when he thanked heaven for little ones.)

"To while away the time I went to a cocktail party given by a woman I knew slightly. When the other guests had left, she indicated that she would not resent any, er, mutual expression of physical affection. But I said that unfortunately, there was no time for that sort of business now, that I had to hurry off to meet my darling at the airport. But, well, she insisted, this very attractive matron, and the next thing I knew I was in her bedroom with the light on, and there was no time for anything elaborate or taking off much clothing. The lady indicated how she liked to be pleasured, and I don't normally go in for that sort of thing much, but what the hell, even if a lady should want bonbons shoved up her ass, old Niven here would be the first to run out to Schrafft's. So there I am on the bed pleasuring the lady in the fashion she enjoyed, light on, and from time to time a surreptitious looking at my watch and thinking of my darling, Hjordis, when I suddenly get the awful feeling that I'm being watched, you know that feeling? I lift up my head, and there in the doorway is her eleven-year-old daughter, and so help me, after all my years in acting and improvisation, all I can think of to say at that moment is, 'Mummy's lost an earring, and I'm helping her look for it!'"

The next time I saw David was at "The Grove," the yearly Bohemian Club encampment near Santa Rosa, California, when he was the guest of William F. Buckley, Jr. Deep in the thousand-year-old redwood forest, David told innumerable stories around the campfire. Though most of his tales lose in the retelling because of David's superb powers of mimicry and the variety of accents he employed, I remember one about a Yorkshire sergeant he knew.

"The regiment was very excited because this day the Queen was going to review the troops. They had prepared for weeks to be letter *perfect*, but as the Queen started walking down the line of men, nodding graciously at each, a burly private in the front line broke wind. It was not a simple breakage, but a prolonged, trombone-like, stentorian epic with no sign of abatement that threatened to disrupt the entire solemn affair. As the sergeant yanked the abashed soldier out of the line to hustle him off to the brig, the Yorkshireman was heard to mutter at the culprit, 'Naow tha shall not see nao fookin' queen!'"

Winston Churchill once said that the three hardest things to do were to climb a wall leaning toward you, kiss a girl leaning away from you, and give an after-dinner speech. David could certainly do the last two with ease. One of his favorite misadventures that he liked telling about after dinner occurred when he was making the film *The Pink Panther* in the Italian Alps.

An ardent skier, one day he ignored the fact that the weather was turning cold and that no one else was going up to the top of the mountain. When he began skiing down, it was 35 degrees below zero. He was dressed in light pants, and halfway down he suddenly "got a feeling of absolutely nothing in precisely the spot where I should have been the warmest . . . something had gone wrong amidships—*frostbite*."

He reached the bottom of the hill in great pain, and the experts commanded, "Alcohol! We must put it in alcohol quickly!"

David was driven to the elegant resort of Cortina d'Ampezzo, whisked into the bar of the Hotel de La Poste, and a large brandy glass was filled with whiskey.

"In the lavatory, while the Italians formed a solicitous, clucking semicircle, I faced the agony of the thaw and pried out of my ski pants a pale-blue acorn. Into the whiskey it went, and the pain was excruciating. This moment was chosen by a smart Milanese nobleman, whom I happened to know, to enter with a view of relieving himself. He took in the tableau at a glance.

"'David,' he asked in a horrified voice, 'what *are* you doing?'

"'I'm pissing in a brandy glass,' I muttered between clenched teeth. 'I always do.'"

More from David: "I've always loved the story about my friend Evelyn Waugh, that old curmudgeon, when he heard that Randolph Churchill, Winston's no-good son, had been operated upon. A tumor on his alimentary canal was found to be benign. 'What a pity,' sniffed Waugh, 'to remove the one part of Randolph that is not malignant.'"

The last time I saw David he was not well. I asked him if he were going back to Spain, where he and I had once enjoyed such a good time.

"No," he said wistfully. "I am a stay-at-home these days, but, you know, rather enjoying it. I'm like that elderly butler that Henry Green, the novelist, told about. When asked what he most liked in the world, the old boy replied: 'Lying in bed on a summer morning, with the window open, listening to the church bells, eating buttered toast with cunty fingers.'"

And he added, "That's me to a tee!"

Songwriter Howard Dietz once remarked that a day away from Tallulah Bankhead was like a month in the country. In the Mat we found that out, over and over.

Once a great actress and star of radio, TV, and films (*The Little Foxes, Skin of Our Teeth*), Tallulah was a scandalous and a startling beauty (Augustus John's portrait of her in London's Tate Gallery captures this superbly). When I met her in El Matador in the late fifties, though, she had become a parody of herself. A tiny woman with an unusually large head, she would sweep theatrically into the bar, her too-long hair swirling around that lovely ravaged face, bellowing for a drink and followed by two or three sycophantic young men. Her pale and perfect skin always made me think of John Cheever's heroine who "was a pretty woman with that striking pallor you so often find in nymphomaniacs." She was always a pleasant, sexy, friendly drunk, and that unique and frequent throaty laugh would cheer the whole room. She loved to talk and rarely stopped. Someone once said, "Talloo starts talking the moment she hears footsteps!"

She was in town for a long run of Noel Coward's play *Private Lives* ("My God, we've played this show everywhere except under water."), and she would come into the Mat after the show. She would drape herself over the piano bar, flirt with pianist John Horton Cooper, and sing along with him. "Dahling, play 'I'll Be Seeing You' again, you swarthy beauty!"

That voice! Critic John Crosby wrote that it had "more timbre than Yellowstone National Park."

There is an old show biz story about Talloo on the first day of rehearsals of what would become one of her great stage triumphs. At the end of the first run-through, a brash young actor in the play approached the star and blurted out, "Miss Bankhead, before the end of the run of this play, I intend to fuck you!"

Tallulah is supposed to have looked him over with those large and sensuous eyes and murmured, "And so you shall, you sweet talkin' possum, so you shall."

One night in El Matador, emboldened by a drink or two, I asked Tallulah if the anecdote were true.

"Dahling, all the outrageous stories about me are true."

"And did he?"

"Of course." She smiled at the memory. "Sweet talkin' possum that he was!"

Another night, she volunteered stories about when she starred in the classic movie *Lifeboat*. The entire film takes place in a lifeboat at sea. The producer wanted music on the track, but the director, Alfred Hitchcock, protested. "There goes the realism. The boat's in the middle of the ocean—tell me where the damn music would be coming from?" And the producer countered with, "I'll tell you where the damn music's coming from if you tell me where the damn camera's coming from!"

· There are many Talloo stories, but I like this one a writer friend of mine tells about making *Lifeboat.* One day the cameraman came to the director in consternation. "Hitch," he whispered all upset, "Talloo isn't wearing any underpants. What the hell will I do?" And good old Hitch replied in his throaty rumble, "Well, wot would you have me do—would you have me call wardrobe, makeup, or the hairdresser?"

She loved baseball and she loved San Francisco. "There have been only two geniuses in this world," she said. "Willie Shakespeare and Willie Mays."

Brendan Gill has written of her: "She *was* different, and not alone in respect to her talent and vitality. She flailed about in paroxysms of disguised bewilderment, drinking and clowning and cursing and showing off. She was valiant and silly, and she knew it. But she was not rubbishy, and she knew that, too. Out of exceptional qualities, she invented by trial and error an exceptional self, which with a child's impudent pretence of not caring she flung straight into the face of the world."

I like what Talloo said one night in the Matador: "If I had my life to live over again, I'd make the same mistakes—only sooner."

Then there was the night that was to be known forever around the Matador as "The Night Saroyan Came In." I wonder how many people read William Saroyan these days, even though his likeness has recently been on the twenty-nine-cent stamp and a huge authorized biography is due to be published. In his day he was big—very big, both as a writer and a personality—although someone once said of William Saroyan's stories that, like those of Henry James, "the author chews more than he bites off."

Nevertheless, the publication in 1934 of Saroyan's first book, *The Daring Young Man on the Flying Trapeze,* made the twenty-six-year-old Armenian-American from Fresno, California, a household word and an international literary sensation.

I met him in 1938 when I was sixteen. My older brother had brought him home to our house in Hillsborough, California. Our parents had gone away for the weekend, had given the two servants time off, and had inadvisedly left us boys in charge. My brother, a Stanford student, had promptly invited a group of girls and boys for a beer bust and paddle tennis on the lawn in front of our big house. (As some wag has remarked, "In the old days, 'safe sex' simply meant that your parents had gone away for the weekend.")

I didn't know who Saroyan was, my reading not having progressed much beyond Kipling, Dickens, and Hemingway, but the first conversation went like this:

"Barnaby—what a wonderful name!" Saroyan had such enthusiasm about everything. "I love that name. Never heard that name."

"Surely you've heard of *Barnaby Rudge,*" I said.

"No," said Saroyan, "who was he?"

"It was a book by Dickens."

"Ah," said Saroyan. "Next year I will read Dickens. Last year it was Tolstoy. This year it is the Oz books. Have you read the Oz books? They are greater than Tolstoy! I am writing a play this week. It is a great play, better than Eugene O'Neill, more life, better characters. I will call my protagonist Barnaby!" (He did, too.)

Later in the afternoon, after a lot of beer, I jumped in the swimming pool with all my clothes on.

"Look at that crazy little fool!" my brother said.

"Not at all," said Saroyan, "he did what he wanted to do at exactly the moment when he wanted to do it!"

Whereupon, clad in his only suit, a shiny black one, and ski boots, which he always wore though he'd never been skiing, he too jumped in the pool, forcing him to spend the night until his clothes were dry the next day.

I didn't see Bill again for many years, until one night at El Matador. One of our best bartenders was a young man named Bill Edison. Of the St. Louis shoe manufacturing clan, Bill was a *cum laude* graduate from Amherst. I asked him why he'd come to San Francisco to become a bartender. "Saroyan," he answered. "I saw *The Time of Your Life*. He's my favorite writer. But this sure isn't much like the play, and I think I'll go back to St. Louis."

Since Edison was a fine fellow as well as our best bartender, I kept hoping Saroyan himself would come in and make it all wonderful for the young man so that he would stay. But though many writers of stature came in quite regularly, such as Erskine Caldwell, Budd Schulberg, John Steinbeck, and Irwin Shaw, Saroyan wasn't among them. I'd heard that he'd long since left San Francisco and was living in Paris. It became an almost sad running gag between Edison and me:

"Think Saroyan'll come in tonight?"

"Suuure—tonight's the night!"

Then, one spring night, one miraculous night, in walked, unannounced, the mustachioed, side-chopped, graying, ebullient author.

He looked around the room, spread his arms wide, and boomed, "What a marvelous place—I like it, I admire it, I esteem it, I love it!"

He gave me a big hug, asked about my brother and my life, and told me about the play he'd written using my name for one of the characters. I started to take him to the bar to meet Bill Edison when I remembered—my god—it was Bill's day off! I phoned his house, and the baby-sitter said he was at the movies. I sent my manager in a cab to extract him and went back to Saroyan. Since the movie house was a long way away, I bought Saroyan a bottle of champagne and had the piano player play all his favorite tunes to keep him entertained. Then, just as Saroyan was leaving, Bill rushed in and I introduced the ecstatic young man. Saroyan stayed, and Bill impressed the author with his insights and encyclopedic knowledge of Saroyan's writing, and they talked far into the night about their favorite subject: Saroyan.

"He was great," said Bill later. "It made it all worthwhile." And he stayed on as my best bartender, later going on to a distinguished career in the California school system.

Although Saroyan had known great success and had won the Pulitzer Prize at the age of thirty-two, his life was never as carefree as his writing or the optimistic image he strove so hard to project suggested. As a child, he had spent five years in an orphanage, and in 1943, the year of his most popular book, *The Human Comedy,* he married a beautiful and witty eighteen-year-old debutante whose bleak childhood was similar to his own. Carol Marcus, an illegitimate child, had been boarded in a series of foster homes until she was eight. The marriage was a disaster, and the two married and divorced each other twice in eight years. Carol subsequently married actor Walter Matthau, but Bill lived alone for the rest of his nomadic life.

I received Saroyanesque letters from him, but I never saw him again. He was going to come to our writers' conference in Santa Barbara in 1981, but then he learned he had cancer and only a short time to live. He died at the age of seventy-two, bitter and disillusioned. His son, Aram, said he left a will that effectively disinherited both his sister and himself, its terms perpetuating the cycle of abandonment, "orphaning two succeeding generations as he had been orphaned."

When Saroyan learned of his fatal condition, he was puzzled and told the press, "I always knew people must die, but I thought in my case an exception would be made. Now what?"

Aram went to see him just before he died.

"I'm letting go," Saroyan said at one point during the visit. "Well, somebody said maybe that's not the right thing to do. And I said, 'Maybe it isn't. I don't know. I'm grappling with the mystery of . . . what . . . *is*.'"

And then it was like the end of his most famous story, *The Daring Young Man on the Flying Trapeze:*

> Then, swiftly, neatly, with the grace of the young man on the trapeze, he was gone from his body. For an eternal moment he was all things at once: the bird, the fish, the rodent, the reptile, and man. An ocean of print undulated endlessly and darkly before him. The city burned. The herded crowd rioted. The earth circled away, and knowing that he did so, he turned his lost face to the empty sky and became dreamless, unalive, perfect.

And William Saroyan himself had become unalive and perfect.

One night Eva Gabor came into the Matador when she was touring in Noel Coward's play *Nude with Violin*. We fell in love. Like that. She came in every night after that.

Eva was always delightfully enthusiastic and less cynical than her famous sister, Zsa Zsa, who said to Herb Caen once, "Shortly after I marry George Sanders—vun veek to be exact—I discover vee haf only vun thing in common: I am in love with George and George iss in love with George."

And: "Vy you men always make such beeg deal about adultery? Dahling, vee women know that vee just take a shower and vee good as new!"

Eva was not at all like that. Eva was single, and I was separated from my wife at the time, and we saw each other for many months in San Francisco and Los Angeles. But there was no talk of marriage; an incurable romantic, I thought one of these fine evenings into El Matador would walk Miss Right. I had a while to wait.

One night after the show, Eva brought with her the Master himself, Noel Coward. Eva urged him to take over the piano from our regular pianist, and he did.

"Oh dear me, this piano," he said, striking a chord. "It fights back."

Nevertheless, he played and sang for an hour, punctuating his songs—"Zigeuner," "I'll See You Again," "Mad Dogs and Englishmen"—with acerbic comments that had the people seated at nearby tables in hysterics. He told of the telegram he'd sent his lifelong pal, the great actress Gertrude Lawrence, when she'd finally married her producer and become Mrs. Aldrich.

"Dear Mrs. A—Hooray Hooray Hooray! At last you are deflowered. Your friend, Noel Coward."

And he'd received a wire back from her: "Dear Mr. C—you know me, my parts I overact 'em. As for the flowers, the maid she must have packed 'em."

Then there was this brief exchange between Eva Gabor and my brother, Hunt, who had lost a leg in a Montana rodeo and wore a prosthesis.

Eva: "Bahnaby tells me you haf a vooden leg." She groped under the table. "Vhich vun iss it, may I ask?"

Hunt: "Eva, I never thought I'd have to tell a Gabor what a man's leg feels like."

Eva (a little loftily): "Vell, dahling, ve vass never in the lumber business!"

When I knew her in the fifties, Eva Gabor was not as well known as her sister, Zsa Zsa, but she was prettier, sharper, and nicer. I was crazy about her. I loved the way she talked, her accent, her little malapropisms. She spoke of her first husband as being "so unscrewable"—it took me a while to figure out she meant inscrutable.

In 1958, I was badly gored in El Escorial, Spain, while performing in a festival fight; the animal's horn went in nine inches, traversing the upper part of my left leg. As I lay in critical condition in the hospital, the following dialogue took place in Sardi's restaurant in New York. It was recorded by columnist Leonard Lyons:

Eva Gabor (as she enters and sees Noel Coward at a table): "Noel dahling, have you heard the news about poor Bahnaby? He vass terribly gored in Spain!"

Noel (genuinely alarmed): "He was what?"

Eva: "He vass gored!"

Noel (genuinely relieved): "Thank heavens—I thought you said bored."

José Ferrer came into the Matador several times, but I did this life-size charcoal of the distinguished actor in his dressing room in the San Francisco theater where he was performing in *The Sunshine Boys*. I was fascinated, as you can see, by all the tubes and jars and brushes that went into transforming him into Neil Simon's old vaudevillian. Joe was an extraordinarily versatile man: trained as an architect at Princeton, he was a fine draughtsman and cartoonist, as well as a singer, pianist, director, comedian, and, of course, stage and film actor par excellence. Although acclaimed for his roles in *The Shrike, Charley's Aunt, Othello,* and *Lawrence of Arabia,* he will probably always be known for his Oscar-winning Cyrano de Bergerac.

Opening Night   Barnaby Conrad 1974

I first met Joe in 1952 when he and John Huston bought the film rights of my novel *Matador.* The two of them had just finished *Moulin Rouge,* a big hit, and were hoping to repeat their success. Although the movie of *Matador* was never made, Joe and I became friends. He had a marvelous sense of humor, and a luncheon with him was like a visit to the Algonquin's famed Round Table. He told great stories about his friends, imitating them to perfection, but his best impression was of the late, great eccentric, his favorite director, John Huston. Here's one of their "small adventures":

"We were walking down a New York street one spring morning, and we see a small crowd around a prostrate elderly man on the sidewalk. Good old John always has to take charge of everything, so he steps forward in a brisk official way and parts the group like Moses parting the Red Sea: 'Shay, whatsh going on here?'" José mimicked Huston's booming and commanding sibilance perfectly.

"Well, the poor old guy is out. He's blue and a goner and rigor mortis is already setting in, but John kneels down, puts his ear to the man's chest, lays his hand on the marble-cold forehead, stands up with that big god-like smile, and, before walking on, announces to the crowd, 'He's going to be fine, folks, jush fine!'"

The night Richard Burton came into the Matador I happened to be out of town, which I always regretted. But we subsequently became friends, mainly because of a song.

My first wife and I had gone to Spain in 1949 on our honeymoon, stayed at the sprawling old Hotel Santa Clara in Torremolinos, and ended up running the lovely seaside resort for six weeks while the owners went on their vacation. In the musty bar of the hotel was an upright piano with a single piece of sheet music on it, entitled "Dream of Olwyn." I played it and played it again and fell in love with the haunting, old-fashioned melody. I couldn't stop playing it. After we left, I never heard it anywhere.

Years later, in 1963, my present wife, Mary, and I went to the jungle village of Mismaloya, near Puerto Vallarta, where I was to write a magazine article on the making of the film *Night of the Iguana*. Near the elaborate set, John Huston introduced us to Elizabeth Taylor, who was drinking a preprandial margarita in the morning sun by the pool. Not far away was a makeshift, thatched cantina set up for the film crew, and I went to get us something to drink. Coming in from the glare, I couldn't see much and thought that, except for the bartender, the place was empty. As I ordered two margaritas, I heard someone at the end of the bar whistling a tune—it was "Dream of Olwyn." As my eyes became accustomed to the gloom, I saw that the whistler was Richard Burton, sitting alone over a drink.

"Doctor Livingston," said that unmistakable voice, "I presume."

I introduced myself and remarked about the song; he said it was his favorite, and I believe he said it came from an early film of his. He was delighted that someone else knew it.

He was very friendly and totally charming. "Call me Rich—Dick sounds too much like an appendage."

As Lauren Bacall once said, "Bogie loved him. We all did. You had no alternative."

We had a margarita together, and over the next week we had many more—what a storyteller, what a wicked mimic, what a delightful drinking companion.

During that week, spent mostly in the cantina, he loved to sprinkle his conversation with Shakespeare and Welsh expressions, and one morning he combined them by reciting to me and the Mexican bartender the "To be or not to be" soliloquy in Welsh. Even though every word was incomprehensible, that amazing voice of his made it strangely moving. Rich was delighted when the bartender countered with his version in Spanish: "*Ser o no ser, eso si es el problema . . .* "

Burton immediately imitated the bartender's rendition in flawless Spanish to the man's amazement and delight. Burton didn't know the language—he simply had an incredible ear.

He told me of doing Hamlet once in England and seeing Winston Churchill in one of the front stalls, "muttering the lines right along" with him.

"Damn disconcerting, I can tell you. Then he comes backstage and says,"—here a perfect imitation of Churchill—"M'lord Hamlet, may I use your facilities?"

He loved theater stories, and he had an inexhaustible supply.

Once in a play with the intimidating John Gielgud, a young messenger approached with news crucial to the plot. "One look at the imperious Gielgud and the kid dried up, went blank, zero, nothing, nada. Gielgud was forced to ad-lib, if the play was going to continue, 'Varlet, hast thou naught to say?' Came a long, long pause. Then finally and weakly from the messenger, 'Naught, m'lord.'"

Burton would chuckle as he savored "the good old days," such as the many ones involving his friend Michael Redgrave.

"In this one play, we worked up to the dramatic scene where Michael is supposed to do himself in. What he was supposed to say at the climactic curtain was, 'Bring me a pint of port and a pistol.' What came out as clear as a bell was, 'Bring me a pint of piss and a portal.' The young actor tried valiantly to save the day! 'A pint of *piss*, m'lord?' Redgrave rallied desperately: 'Aye, you dolt,' he shouted, '*and* a portal!'"

But his best story is the St. David's Day Debacle:

"March first is St. David's Day, and no Welshman ever works on our greatest holiday, no matter what. Therefore,

I was astonished when I get a call from the stage manager saying where the hell are you—we've a performance tonight. And I said, You're bloody out of your mind, it's St. David's Day and I've been drinkin' ale since nine this bloody morning and I'm not even sure of my sainted mother's name. And they say, Get your Welsh ass down here to the theater or else! So I somehow stagger down there, they pour me into the armor before I've even had a chance to go to the bathroom, and they shove me clanking out onto the stage with Redgrave. Luckily, I don't have a lot to say in the act, but there's lots of standing around, and I have to take the most fierce piss, and there's no way I can leave the stage. And oh god, Shakespeare goes on and on, and Redgrave goes on and on, and it's awful, but I just come to a point where I can't hold all that ale a second longer, and I let go. I feel it running down my legs, and I see it spurtin' out at my knees above the greaves, and oh god it's awful. As I see it pool around m' feet and in my frustration, since I'm supposed to kill Redgrave, the king, I raise my wooden sword and bring it down on the poor bastard's shoulder, and the sword breaks off, and I'm left with just the hilt. I sure as hell can't kill him with that, so I rush at him, and poor Redgrave is looking terrified as he sees this great Welsh bull charging down on him, and as I grab him by the crotch and hoist him high up to throw him over the hedge, he sings out a wail that the whole theater hears, 'Mind m'balls, mind m'balls!'"

Burton chuckled at the memory and drank. "Never thought I'd ever work again after *that!*"

About the big scandal when the press got wind of the secret romance between him and Elizabeth Taylor, which started on the set of *Cleopatra* in Rome, he remarked, "We just got fed up with all the hiding from the press, the hypocrisy, and the pretence. Finally, I said to Liz, 'Fuck it, let's go out to fuckin' Alfredo's and have some fuckin' fettucine.'"

In Mismaloya, he and Elizabeth made no effort to hide their affection for each other. One day he called to her tenderly across the swimming pool in that most romantic of masculine voices, "Darling, there's not a single part of you that I don't know," (pause) "remember," (pause) "and *want!*"

She blinked her eyes, threw a kiss to him. "How sweet," she said, "How terribly, terribly sweet, my darling."

Rich smiled and said to me under his breath, "Poor little baggage will never know that Noel Coward wrote that line a long, *long* time ago."

A little while later a beautiful Mexican girl slinked by him in a bathing suit made up of little more than three Band-Aids and some string. *"Tantas curvas y yo sin frenos!"* said Richard in a line he'd learned from the bartender. "So many curves and me without brakes!"

Elizabeth glared at him. "Richard!"

Richard shrugged in apology and said, "Just because I own the Mona Lisa, am I not allowed to look at the other pictures in the exhibition?"

Elizabeth beamed lovingly at him.

What a way Richard had with women of any age! I like the story John Huston used to tell about him: "Someone asked Raymond Massey if there was *any* woman Burton hadn't managed to seduce. 'Yes,' the actor said solemnly, 'Marie Dressler.' 'But she's dead!' the other replied. 'Yes, I know,' said Massey."

When John Wayne came into the Matador it was big excitement. Even the blasé waiters jumped and vied for the honor of waiting on his table.

"Escosés y soda, a-meeg-oh," Wayne said to José, the waiter, in that world-renowned drawl. Duke was married to a Peruvian woman, was a friend of matador Carlos Arruza, and was a great bullfighting aficionado. He prided himself on his Spanish, which was terrible.

After signing a few autographs, usually forbidden in my place, he said to me casually, "Listen, pilgrim, I reread that book, *Matador*, of yours, and I want to make a film of it; I'll have my agent call you tomorrow."

"Wonderful," I said. "Who do you see in the lead?"

There was a Wagnerian silence.

"Who," he said finally in steely and measured tones, "who do I see in the lead?"

At that point, Duke was fifty, balding, and heavy, and I couldn't believe that he saw himself in the role of a lithe bullfighter. When I realized the extent of my gaffe, I tried to recover as best I could, stammering, "I meant the *second* lead—the manager."

I don't think I fooled him, and I knew I would never hear from his agent, but he was soon friendly again. He had another scotch and suggested we go to see the matador Arruza perform in Tijuana the following Sunday.

At one point, he got up and went to the bathroom. He came back in a few minutes with one of his gabardine pants legs wet. As he asked the bartender for a towel, he said, "Always happens when I go to a public restroom." He sighed resignedly. "The guy doing his business in the urinal next to me sees me, swivels around, and exclaims, 'Hey, you're John Wayne,' and wets my leg. Never fails."

Ah—the damp price of fame.

John Dodds, the New York publisher, came into the Matador on his wedding night. He'd just married Vivian Vance, Lucille Ball's sidekick Ethel Mertz on "I Love Lucy." During the evening he said to me, "I'm going to give you a large hunk of dough to write a book!"

John wanted me to write the memoirs of the culinary curmudgeon Victor Bergeron, "Trader Vic" to the restaurant-going public, for what seemed an inordinate amount of money.

I should have listened to another visitor to the Matador, Norman Mailer, who once said, "I've never written a book because there's going to be a lot of money in it, because I know that's the surest way to take five years off your life."

That night John explained the large advance this way: "Everyone's dying to know about this great restaurateur. People know his Polynesian food, they know his mai tais and fog cutters, but they don't know the man, they don't know his private life, his fascinating background as a South Seas trader, how he lost his leg—I think it was a shark—his two wives, his celebrity friends, and so forth. He'll trust you because you're a painter, and he's a would-be artist."

Unlike the many cookbooks by him about his exotic dishes, this was to be an intimate, as-told-to affair about his rise from a little greasy spoon called Hinky Dink's in Oakland, California, to San Francisco's most stylish restaurant, a growing empire with branches in Hawaii, Los Angeles, New York, and London.

I was to meet with him every day in his office in the San Francisco Trader Vic's, the flagship restaurant, and record conversations with him about his life, his philosophy, his family, and his expertise with food. I would then distill, edit, and embellish the material. From the very first day, I knew it was going to be a tough assignment. I was greeted by Shep, the elegant doorman, and went through the main entrance of the restaurant, a mélange of huge clam shells, fish nets, native drums, a ship's brass annunciator, and a shrunken human head in a glass case.

"Right this way, sir," said the maître d', showing me to a side room. "Mr. Bergeron will be here shortly." I was sitting in Vic's small office waiting for him, lulled by taped Hawaiian music, when the sixty-five-year-old man clumped in from the kitchen past the exotic Chinese ovens on his artificial leg. A powerfully built man, he was wearing his ubiquitous black turtleneck.

"I'll tell ya!" he roared, sitting down heavily behind his *koa* wood desk and slapping his prosthesis. "Don't get one of these goddamn things unless you really need it!"

I didn't ask about his leg. I didn't have to. The information came out immediately—he hadn't lost his leg romantically to South Sea pirates, or in the war, or in a shark attack in the Marquesas Islands, as variously reported by different press agents. The truth was he'd fallen off "a goddamn lumber pile" when he was six years old in Alameda, California, where he grew up. He'd contracted osteomyelitis, and the leg was taken off at the hip.

"But to hell with all that," he said. Then abruptly: "Okay, here's a cute one." He chuckled in anticipation. "This is the answer: Penis Rabinowitz."

I shook my head.

"The question is: What was Cock Robin's real name?" He guffawed and smote his prosthesis, which resounded hollowly like a Tahitian log drum. "Penis Rabinowitz!"

Behind him on several shelves were just some of the dozens of items developed by Trader Vic's—everything from chocolate coffee to salad dressings to coconut oil. The by-products of Trader Vic's had long since become an even bigger source of revenue than the restaurants. Desperate for some color for the story, I asked him what he did before he went into the restaurant business.

"Sold paint at Fuller's paint store," he said. "I could really mix paint—match any color you wanted, right on the button. I knew I had some talent right then."

He pointed. On the wall was his latest painting, which he had just varnished: a cheerful, overframed scene in bright colors depicting a group of nuns clamming on a beach. It looked as though it had been done by a latter-day Grandma Moses. It had some charm and I told him so.

"I like that one a lot, too" he said, admiring it. "Real cute."

His secretary called in: "Mr. Bergeron, line one—it's Herb Caen."

"I get a kick," Vic said. "He always calls me 'Trade.' I get a kick."

After talking to the newspaper columnist for a few minutes, he hung up and said, "He wanted to know if it was true that I was designing a new menu for United Airlines. You're goddamn right it's true. But I'm not about to tell him that. And don't you print it either, till I tell you."

An old Chinese waiter brought in two rum mai tais and put the frosted glasses in front of us. "I invented this drink one day several years ago," he said. "Had a Tahitian friend try it. She tasted it, and said, 'ooo, mai tai, mai tai!' That means 'good' in Tahitian, so we named it that. It's good for the bowels."

I told him I'd spent some time in Tahiti and asked how long he'd lived in the South Seas.

"Shee-yit," he said. "I went to Tahiti last year for the first time, and I hated the goddamn place! Here all these years I've been promoting South Seas cuisine and South Seas products, and I go there and see it for myself, and it rains all the time and the girls have bad teeth and the food is crummy and I can't wait to leave. It's the pits. It's a boil on the ass of creation that place, I'll tell ya!"

He sipped his mai tai and belched. "Know something? I've never been drunk in my life. I drink every day, but I'm the only person I've ever known who's never been drunk. You ever meet anyone who's never been drunk?"

"My grandfather," I said. Then I plunged in. "Speaking of families, what was yours like?"

There was a pause.

"Great mother, great father," he said shiftily. Then he laughed. "Say, what d'ya get when you cross a mule with an onion? Well, mostly you just get an onion with big ears, but every once in a while you get a piece of ass that brings tears to your eyes." And again he slapped his false leg in enjoyment. "Cute, eh?" He laughed again and repeated the punch line. "Love a cute story. Don't like those crude ones."

"Oh, Boss," his secretary called in. "Forgot to tell you Bing called. He says he can't sing at your charity lunch—out of town."

"Shee-yit," said Vic, slapping the desk. He looked at me. "That guy is a very strange man, that Crosby guy. Him and that lah-dee-dah wife."

"Speaking of wives," I said, "what year did you and your first wife start Hinky Dink's?"

His expression changed. He reached over and turned off the tape recorder. "Now let's get this straight!" he said in a low voice. "We gotta get this straight: No mention of her in this book, understan'?"

"But—" I protested. "You started Hinky Dink's together! You have those four kids!"

"Hinky Dink's," he mused and smiled at the name.

He looked up at the ceiling. "Yeah, she was great. She'd wait on tables, clean the place, clean the toilets. I'd cook, flip fried eggs over a beam and catch 'em. Right over this big old beam! People'd come in the place just to see me do that." Then he said, "Okay, you can mention the kids, but absolutely no mention of her. Prim, my present wife, she'd go through the roof."

"But, where do I say the kids came from?" I asked.

"That's your problem," he said. Then he brightened. "Hey, this guy walks into a bar, see, has a penguin on his shoulder ... "

The old Chinese waiter came in with a tray. On it were six plates with three versions of a new Trader Vic rice and squab recipe.

"Trying out a new curry dish for United," he said, as the waiter put three plates in front of him and three in front of me. Each had a number. Vic took a forkful of number one and stared at the ceiling as he rolled it around in his mouth. Then number two and three. I did the same as the waiter watched expectantly.

"Which one do you like?" he said.

"Number three," I said.

"Number three?" he asked incredulously. "You don't know shit from shinola." He turned to the waiter. "Tell cheffie numbah one," he said. "Numbah one mo' bettah." Back to me. "Jeez, you don't know anything about food, do you?"

As the waiter gathered up the plates and left the room, Vic said with affection in his voice, "That waiter just left? Y'know, that little guy's been with me for thirty-five years! Was with me over in Oakland, too. Thirty-five goddamn years!"

"What's his name?" I asked.

"His name is . . . " Vic frowned. Then he bellowed at his secretary in the outer office, "Hey Liz, what the hell's the name of that little Chinaman that just left the office?"

"Lum," the secretary called back. "Henry Lum, Mr. Bergeron."

"Yeah," said Vic, unabashed. "That's it, Lum. Great little guy. He has stock in my restaurants. I give 'em all stock, that's why they stay, why they work so hard. They're partners. Say, have you heard the one about the black hooker and the big dog and the box of Alpo? Goes like this . . . "

"Mr. Bergeron, line two," Liz called out. "It's Mrs. Bergeron."

Vic picked up his phone. "Hi, Prim." His voice went soft now. "Yes, dear. *How* many people? Jeez, that's a lot of people! I know it's an important charity but . . . " He listened, for a long time. "Yes, dear, I'll start setting it up. G'bye, Prim."

He slammed down the phone. "Am I the *only* source of charity in this cheap town?" He stared down at his desk. "Women. It's lucky they got a pussy or there'd be a bounty on 'em. But you know what—they got kind of a tough lot. Jeez, they have to worry about kids and food and the servants and the garden and then the old man comes home with a couple of drinks in him and wants to crawl on their body. They really don't have it all that easy." He brooded for a while, then brightened. "Anyway, there's this guy invites a hooker up to his apartment and . . . "

After several sessions almost exactly like the first one, I grew quite depressed. I found I could not write this book. There was nothing to write about, except recipes. But I hated to give back the advance, so I hired a ghost writer. People thought it was funny—a ghost writer hiring a ghost writer—but the humor escaped me. It turned out terribly. Though a fine journalist, he had done years in the pen for extortion, and he and Vic were old enemies; he could hardly wait to give Vic the shaft in print. "Not only that, I'm saying a whole lot of terrible things about myself in the book," the writer told Herb Caen, "so then when it comes out I can sue the hell out of him!"

Vic found out about the writer.

"That con man, that sleaze, that blackmailer! You're working with *him!?* Why—he's the fingernail down the blackboard of life, that guy!"

Disaster. The project was dropped summarily, and I was in the doghouse with everyone.

But I had some fantastic lunches and I heard a lot of jokes. A lot of bad jokes.

I used to go almost every night to the Hungry i to catch Don Asher, the pianist, or Mort Sahl, or Woody Allen when he was just starting. Woody was unknown then, and though he was a very nervous stand-up comic, he was very funny. This routine about his ex-wife quickly spread around North Beach: "She was coming home late at night, and she was violated. That's how they put it in the New York papers: she was violated. And they asked me to comment on it. I said, 'Knowing my ex-wife, it probably was not a moving violation.'"

And his classic story of shooting a moose that later comes to on the car's fender defies the written word but causes a chuckle in the memory of anyone who ever heard it.

I went back to the Matador this particular night and tried to recount Woody's routine to Joe Rosenthal, but he was too excited to listen. Joe is a small, self-effacing man, and he took what is probably the most famous WWII photograph, the raising of the U.S. flag on Mount Suribachi on Iwo Jima.

"I'm going to Washington, D.C., tomorrow," he said. "They're unveiling the statue that they've made from my photo! They say it's huge, maybe fifty feet high!"

Joe, characteristically, has never made a dime off that great photo, refusing every offer and attempt to commercialize it. Not only has he chosen not to make money from the photo, but it has cost him thousands of dollars over the years, since he has honored every request for a print of it and paid for the costs out of his modest salary from the *San Francisco Chronicle*. Painfully shy, he has always shunned the limelight. But this statue was different; he was thrilled.

"I'm going to take my wife and kids," he said. "And the survivors of the guys who actually raised the flag are going to be there, too!"

Three days after the unveiling, which garnered great publicity, Joe was back and in the Matador. Uncharacteristically, he seemed very down.

"How'd it go?" I asked.

"Great," he said. But I noticed he was drinking doubles.

Little by little, the story came out. At the unveiling, the tarpaulin was dropped, revealing the huge, lifelike statue of the six marines struggling to raise the flag pole, and a cheer went up. Joe and his family were in the front of the big crowd.

"Was it like your photo?"

"Exactly," said Joe morosely. "Couldn't have been more like it."

"So?"

So, one of his children pointed out that while the name of the sculptor, Felix de Weldon, was in large letters on the base, nowhere was Joe's name or photo mentioned. And in the many speeches, no credit was given to the combat photographer who had taken the picture that had inspired the sculpture.

It couldn't have happened to a nicer guy, but it all ended happily. A group of us in the bar fired off telegrams to everyone in the government that we could think of, from the president on down. Several weeks later the error was corrected, and now on the base of the much-admired statue is a large plaque reading: "Based on the photograph by Joe Rosenthal."

The night we got the news, drinks at the Matador were on the house.

A rtie Shaw came into El Matador, but he doesn't drink and doesn't really like night clubs, considering them, as Hemingway once said, to have only one redeeming feature—as "a place to meet complaisant women."

I didn't really get to know the great bandleader of the Swing Era until some time later at a party.

I play the worst kind of piano, and my friend Malcolm Alexander, the distinguished sculptor, plays only a little better on his battered tenor sax, but we like nothing better than to get together and play for an hour or two. We both play by ear, so I generally think of a tune, any tune,

and start playing it, always in F, and Malcolm "chases" the melody a beat or two behind. Occasionally, undiscriminating friends permit us to play at their parties.

Thus it came to pass that one night we were playing our hearts out at a cocktail party at an artist's friend's studio when for some reason it occurred to me to swing into "Begin the Beguine." This, of course, is the Cole Porter standard made famous for all time by Artie Shaw and his orchestra back in the thirties and forties.

I like the song and was really putting my soul into it, and Malcolm was playing wonderful Coleman Hawkins–type runs, when right in the middle of the bridge Malcolm stopped cold.

"Hey!" I said, continuing to play the song, "what's the matter? Keep going, big finish coming up!"

Silence. I looked up. Malcolm was staring transfixed at someone. It was life's darkest moment. Standing squarely in front of us was Artie Shaw, himself, looking at us with those steely musician's eyes, the eyes of one of the greatest jazz geniuses of all time. The man had a quizzical frown on his face.

Malcolm took the sax out of his mouth, gulped, and murmured like a naughty little boy caught in the act, "I'm sorr-ee."

"No, not at all," Mr. Shaw said gently, earnestly, compassionately. "Please continue. It's just, just that I've never heard it, you know, played quite, quite that way before."

But the playing was over and the talking began, and we soon became fast friends.

Artie Shaw isn't as well known today, and people over sixty often have to explain that he wasn't "just a band leader who married a lot." When I was in my teens, he and Benny Goodman were a phenomenon akin to the Beatles. And I expect when the generation of Beatles fans from the 1960s gets older, it will have the same trouble explaining the impact of, and the devotion inspired by, John, Paul, George, and Ringo. Benny Goodman is a more familiar name today perhaps because he kept playing right up into his seventies, while Artie made his clarinet into a lamp—literally—about thirty years ago and "got out of the Artie Shaw business," as he calls it. His recordings are still played today, and previously unreleased records continue to surface for eager fans.

Everyone I knew when I was young was either a Goodman or a Shaw fan, and the battle lines were drawn clearly. At my prep school, fist fights would start over whether Artie's "Begin the Beguine" or Goodman's "Lady Be Good" was the better recording. (With us purists, Glenn Miller wasn't even in the running.) I was an Artie Shaw addict from the time I first heard his recording of "All the Things You Are" (written, incidentally, by Jerome Kern, one of Artie's eight fathers-in-law). Benny certainly had a dazzling technique, but most of us thought Artie had more musicality and innovation, and he aimed for the heart.

And Artie, in a white dinner jacket in front of that great band, was so slick, so darkly handsome, so cool! An intellectual *and* a jazz great! No wonder he got all those swell-looking women. I wanted to be Artie Shaw. We all did.

Of course he doesn't look quite like that now as you can see in the recent sketch I did of him. ("Do I really have those bags under my eyes?")

Artie is now bald, mustachioed, and pushing a trim eighty-three. But he is still a fascinating character, intense, voluble, opinionated, and charismatic. We became good friends immediately and see each other often. People always ask what he's been doing since he quit "the Artie Shaw business." Well, first he went fishing, but whenever Artie does something, he flings himself into it totally. So he didn't just go fishing, he became a master fly fisherman, fishing all over the world with experts, and did little else for four years. Then he shot rifles for several years, becoming a world-class competitive marksman. In his wallet, where most people his age carry pictures of grandchildren, Artie has the paper targets of several near-perfect, "one-hole, fine-shot groups" that won for him in a world competition. Then for years he went into oil and watercolor painting with the same fervor as his other accomplishments.

Now he concentrates full-time on writing, fiction mostly, which he has always loved. He is one of the best-read men I've ever met. He said, "While the other guys in the band fooled around in the waiting and traveling time,

I read." He has published three well-received books and is now completing a monumental novel.

People keep asking if he'll ever go back to music. He said to me recently, "God no, I had that damned clarinet in my mouth sometimes thirteen hours a day. I quit at the top, when audiences refused to accept what I wanted to do musically. Hell, they didn't want to *listen*, they just wanted to dance. I told them why not just get yourself a windshield wiper and an out-of-tune tenor sax playing "Melancholy Baby"? By the way, can you think of many other people who quit when they were at the top of their stardom—besides Greta Garbo and Michael Jordan and Gene Tunney and me? I got so I just couldn't stand all the bullshit, the constant hype and lack of privacy. Final straw came when one day some so-called fan walked up and shook my hand and said, 'I just want to be able to say I shook the hand that held Ava Gardner's tit.' That did it."

Artie came to speak at our writers' conference recently. During the question and answer period, some feckless youth stood up and asked,"Mr. Shaw, you're an intellectual. Why did you marry someone like Ava Gardner?"

Artie looked at him incredulously and replied, "Did you," (a beat) "did you ever *see* Ava Gardner?!"

Later Artie was talking about his seven marriages— "Actually, eight. I was married at nineteen for about ten minutes, but we won't talk about that." He's been married to, among others, the daughter of composer Jerome Kern, to Kathleen Winsor, the author of *Forever Amber*, and to actress Lana Turner. Artie pretended to make light of his marriages. "Jeez, who goes into a marriage with women like Ava Gardner and Lana Turner and expects it to last forever? People are always asking me for advice about marriage—as if I were an expert on it. Hell, it's divorce I'm an expert on!

"People are always talking about how tough divorce is. What's so hard about it? Just pack a bag and call a cab."

Then he grew serious. "And this business of 'you should try sticking it out.' That's crazy! It's like finding yourself on the wrong subway going to some place you don't want to go, and saying, 'Hell, I won't change trains. I'll just stay on till the end of the line.'"

Though technically out of the music business, Artie loves to tell musician stories.

"This new guitarist shows up for a trio gig, and the piano player is waiting around for him to finish tuning up. It goes on and on, and the piano player says, 'Hey, man, hurry it up, will you?' And the guy keeps right on tuning. Finally, the pianist says, 'Geezus, *Segovia* doesn't take that long to tune up!' And the guitarist looks up at him, offended, and says, 'Yeah? Well, maybe *he* don't care!'"

And as he does with everything, Artie analyzed the story: "That's funny, isn't it? The guy never heard of Segovia. Or, has he? Maybe it's even funnier if he knows exactly who Segovia is. Yeah, I think that's funnier."

Artie loved Louis Armstrong. "Louis—never Louie—was always writing letters in his dressing room between shows. Funny letters with lots of parentheses, like 'smile' and 'tee-hee' and 'giggle'. One day, Erroll Garner went by his room, and there was Louis, hunched over the typewriter, pecking away, that knotted handkerchief on his head, and Erroll said, 'What's new, Pops?' And Louis replies without even looking up, 'White folks still in the lead.'" Artie chuckled at the memory. "I loved that guy."

He told another story about the great jazz saxophonist Zoot Sims: "He found himself the star at one of these ponderous conclaves where people discuss jazz and analyze it to death, and some earnest young cat gets up so seriously and says, 'Mr. Sims, sometimes when I see a G seventh I play an E. Is that okay?' Zoot pursed his lips, looked heavenward, and then nodded and said, 'Yeah, E's a *nice* note. I like E.'"

Then he said, "You have no idea what it's like for a creative musician to have to play the same song, same arrangement, over and over, day after day. When we played the Palace in New York, we did eight shows a day, and eight times a day I'd have to do 'Begin the Beguine' note for note exactly the way we recorded it. The fans wouldn't tolerate even a minor variation. The same with 'Frenesi' after it became a huge hit. In 1949, we were playing this long nightclub gig in Chicago, and night after night this prominent guy would come in and ask for 'Frenesi.' 'We just played it,' I'd say. 'Play it again,' he'd say. Dodo, this really good pianist I had at that time, hated that song above all others in this world. 'I swear to God I can't play that song one more time,' he wailed one night. That same night the guy comes in, asks for, demands 'Frenesi.' I shrug and call for 'Frenesi.' Dodo gets up from the piano, slams down the lid, walks out without a word, and is never heard from again. I mean literally, he disappeared forever."

In 1987, a full-length film on Artie's tumultuous and glamorous life won an Oscar for best documentary. In it there was a revealing interview with actress Evelyn Keyes, Artie's last ex-wife (and still a friend). "Artie and I were having an argument one day—we argued a lot—and at one point he said, 'What do you expect me to be, *God?*' And I said, 'Yes, *God!*' He looked at me and said quietly, 'Well, God needs buttering up, too.'" She looked at the camera and said fondly, "Wasn't that nice?"

She said that Artie is a fascinating man but an exacting and exasperating perfectionist. "For example, the pillows on the bed had to be turned just so, open end in—or maybe out, I forget which. And, very, *very* important, the toilet paper roll had to be placed so that it fed off the top, not the bottom." Then she added, not unkindly, "To this day, whenever I see a roll of toilet paper, I think of Artie Shaw."

Ava Gardner, in her autobiography, summed up her marriage to Shaw this way: "Artie and I remained close for years, and I can't say anything against him. He taught me to study, to think, to read. Thanks to Artie, I read *Death in the Afternoon,* which meant I had a little something to talk to Hemingway about, not to mention having a leg up on the bullfighters who entered my life. Of my three husbands, I had the most admiration for Artie. He's impossible to live with, sometimes even to be friends with, but he is a worthwhile human being, an extraordinary man."

Once, in a subdued and rueful mood, Artie gazed at a group of women in the Matador and mused poignantly, "You know, I can go into a crowded room in any part of the world and go unerringly to the one woman who is going to make me the most miserable."

The night Ava Gardner first came into El Matador, she was sober and gorgeous. But two hours later she had snatched a bullfighter's hat off the wall and was doing a torrid, if lurching, flamenco solo on the bar, her skirt hiked up around her waist, while her anonymous escort looked pained and the customers applauded.

Bing Crosby called me one day at El Matador and asked if I had any pull with the Ritz Hotel in Madrid.

"I want to stay there next week when we go to Spain, but they say they won't allow any actors. Never heard of such a thing!"

I called the hotel, one of the most elegant in the world, and talked to the manager. "I regret to say," he sniffed, "that it has been our policy since—well, for quite some time now—not to allow actors or actresses at our hotel."

Then I phoned an influential connection in Madrid, and he sighed and confirmed the ban. "It's been in effect ever since our friend Ava—well . . . "

"Yes?"

"Well, señor, one day she peed in one of those standing ash trays in the lobby. They got quite upset."

I could believe it of Ava. Sober, she was a quiet, considerate, simple beauty from Grabtown, North Carolina.

When she was drinking, people in the bullfighting world called her "Death in the Evening." The last time I saw Ava was a couple of years ago in her elegant London mews house. She hadn't had a drink for six months, and she looked beautiful. She cooked dinner for a dozen people, moving among the artists, actors, and writers graciously, and in general exuding poise and serenity. But I couldn't help thinking of that time in Madrid at Horcher's, one of Europe's top restaurants. That evening she was already loaded, but she was demanding a martini on the rocks.

"And none of your *falsificadas,* none of your phony Spanish gins!"

Many restaurants and bars would take Tanqueray and Beefeaters bottles and refill them with inferior Spanish gin.

"Si, Señorita Gardner," the wary waiter assured her. "I assure you, it will be genuine English gin."

When the waiter arrived with the drink, Ava took one sip and declared, "*Falsificada!* Take it back!"

The waiter protested once, but then humbly brought another martini. Ava took a sip.

"*Falsificada!*" she cried again. "Where's Horcher?"

Old Herr Horcher, in his tuxedo, came bustling over with an old-world, long-suffering sigh. "Fräulein Gardner, I promise you, zis iss made mit genuvine English gin!"

Ava looked up at him skeptically. "We'll see!" she said.

Then she pulled his pants away from his waist with one hand and with the other poured in the offending martini, rocks and all.

Horcher leapt up with a bellow, clutching his groin. "*Rauch mit em!* Out, out, out!"

And so Ava was barred from still another place. Perhaps her favorite place was the Palace Hotel Bar, an elegant mecca for everyone famous who came to Madrid. This incident contributed to her being barred from *that* watering spa as well.

She was holding court there one evening, and someone said something that teed her off—drink made her supersensitive. She drew herself up, looked around the room, and said as regally as she could, "Fuck you all. I'm leaving."

As she started to wobble her way out of the bar, a man hurried over to her. "Miss Gardner, is there anything I can do to help you?" he asked.

"Fuck off, Jack," she directed.

"I beg your pardon? I'm only trying to help. My name is Michener. I'm a writer."

Gardner hesitated a moment. "What did you say your name was?"

"James A. Michener," came his reply.

"And what do your friends call you?"

"My friends call me Jim," said Michener.

"Well, fuck off, Jim!" she said, and swept out, never to return.

Ava died in February 1990 after a long illness, and the next day I had lunch with her ex-husband, Artie Shaw.

"She was so incredibly beautiful," he said sadly. "But she took what God gave her, all those gifts, and tossed them out the window all her life."

Part Three

The patron saint of El Matador was the Spanish bull-fighter Manolete. After all, it was the novelized account of his life and death that had furnished the wherewithal to create the place.

The first thing you saw upon entering the Matador was this full-length oil portrait of Manolete, which I had painted from sketches and photos I'd taken of him seven years earlier in Lima, Peru. I think the portrait captures some of the dignity, pride, and innate sadness of the man who was called by many the greatest matador of his time.

I knew him and cared deeply about him. This is his dramatic story, which I used to tell on Sunday nights at El Matador when we showed taurine films.

The bull's name was Islero, and he was of the Miura strain. The man's name was Manolete, and he was the essence of everything Spanish. They met at the end of August, 1947, when Manolete was just thirty years old. And when it was over, the headlines blared out: "He died killing and he killed dying!"

His story is the embodiment of *la fiesta brava*.

It's hard for Americans to understand why all the fuss about one bullfighter. But he wasn't just a bullfighter to

the Spaniards, he was their only national and international hero.

He looked quixotic. Ugly in photos, cold and hard in the bull ring, he had tremendous magnetism, warmth, and gentle humor among his friends. Once, in Peru, I took a blasé American college girl to watch Manolete during the preparation ceremony before a fight, though she protested she had no interest in a "joker who hurts little bulls."

"Excuse me, señorita, if I don't talk much," he said with his shy smile, as they worried his thin frame into the skintight uniform. "But I am very scared."

After that he didn't say more than ten words to her, but she walked out of the room dazed. "That," she announced, "is the most attractive man in the world."

An hour later he had her weeping with emotion as he calmly let the horns of a giant Fernandini bull graze the gold braid on his costume time after time. The fear he spoke of was nowhere in evidence.

"To fight a bull when you are not scared is nothing," another bullfighter once said. "And to not fight a bull when you are scared is nothing. But to fight a bull when you are scared—that is something."

Manolete told me, "My knees start to quake when I first see my name on the posters, and they don't stop until the end of the season."

But there was never any real end of the season for him. In 1945, for example, he fought ninety-three fights in Spain in six months, about one every other day. That meant body-racking travel, for he would fight in Barcelona one day, Madrid the next, and then maybe Lisbon the day after. He would snatch some sleep in the train or car, and sometimes he had to board a plane with his ring outfit still on. Then followed Mexico's season and Peru's season, and when he got through with those, it was March again and time for the first fights in Valencia. It would have been grueling even for a very strong man, and

Manolete was frail to the point of appearing tubercular. Yet he kept driving, driving.

What, then, made him run? What made him The Best?

Money would have been the obvious reason. In his eight years as a senior matador, he made approximately 4 million American dollars—in the 1940s! In his last years, he was getting as high as $25,000 per fight, about $400 for every minute he performed, and he could fight where, when, and as often as he liked. His yearly income was abetted by such things as a liqueur called Anís Manolete, dolls dressed in costume with his sad face on them, testimonials for cognac ads, songs about him, and a movie called *The Man Closest to Death.*

Yet it wasn't the money; people seldom risk their necks just for money. It was that he needed desperately to be someone—something great.

He was born Manuel Rodríguez in Cordoba, Spain, in 1917, in the heart of the bullfighting country. His great-uncle, a minor-league bullfighter, was killed by a bull, one of the dreaded Miura breed that years later was to kill Manuel. His mother was already the widow of a great matador when she married Manuel's father, also a bullfighter, who went blind and died in the poorhouse when Manuel was five years old.

The family was always hungry and poor. Manuel was a frail child, having had pneumonia when a baby, and could contribute little to his mother's support. But he started carrying a plasterer's hod as soon as he was big enough to tote one.

One of his sisters stood the hunger as long as possible, and then she started making money in a profession even older than bullfighting. This was the secret of the driving force behind Manuel. He never got over it. He resolved to make enough money somehow so that his family would never have to worry again, and to become such an important person that his sister's shame would be forgotten.

Bullfighting is the only way in Spain for a poor boy to become great. Young Manuel decided to become the greatest bullfighter who ever lived.

In his debut, he was clumsy but so brave and obviously trying so hard that the home folks applauded the sad-faced gawk. It was the greatest day of his life. Flushed with success, he and two other boys scraped their money together, formed a team called the Cordovan Caliphs, and set out to make their fortune. They wangled some fighting at night and in cheap fairs. Manolete was almost the comic relief of the outfit. The crowd would laugh at his skinny frame made more awkward by the fancy passes he was trying. His serious, homely face and his earnestness made it all the funnier.

Then came the turning point in his life, for José Camará spotted him. Camará, a bald, dapper little man of thirty-five with omnipresent dark glasses, might have become the greatest bullfighter of all time except for one thing: he was a coward.

When he saw Manolete gawking around a small-town ring, he knew that here was someone who could be everything that he had failed to be. With his expert eye, he saw what the crowd didn't, that the boy wasn't really awkward, but he was trying the wrong passes for his build and personality. Camará figured that with his brains and Manolete's blood they could really go places. He signed up the astonished young man for a long, long contract.

Camará remade Manolete. He took him out to the ranches and showed him what he was doing wrong. He made him concentrate on only the austere classic passes, not on the spinning or cape-twirling ones.

When Camará thought Manolete was ready, he launched his protégé. People didn't appreciate immediately what they were witnessing, but soon they came to realize that here was a revolutionary, a great artist. His repertoire was startlingly limited, but when he did the simple verónica, the cape became a live thing in his hands, and the easy flow of the cloth, the casual way it brought the bull's horns within a fraction of an inch of his legs, was incredibly moving.

If his first year was successful, his second was sensational. It seemed as though Spain had just been waiting for his kind of fighting. His honest and brave style showed up the fakery that the cape-twirlers had been foisting upon the public.

By 1946, he was the king of matadors, and Mexico beckoned him with astronomical contracts, the highest ever paid to a bullfighter. For his first fight in Mexico City, spectators thought they were lucky to get any seat for a hundred dollars. It was the greatest responsibility a matador ever had, and he gave them their money's worth that day until he was badly wounded. Even then, as they were carrying him to the ring infirmary, he regained consciousness, escaped restraining hands, and lurched back into the ring to finish the bull. Then he collapsed.

He went on to fight all over Mexico and South America. When I saw him in Lima, he was exhausted. Most bullfighters can give a top performance one day and then get away with a few safe, easy ones. But not Manolete. To preserve his fabulous reputation, he had to fight every fight as though it were his first time in the Madrid plaza. But the machine was wearing down. Though he was only twenty-nine, he looked forty. He was drinking a lot—not mild Spanish wine but American whiskey.

Even Camará, who enjoyed having his wallet filled through someone else's risks, thought it was time to quit. But the public makes an idol, tires of what it has made, and destroys the idol. When Manolete returned to Spain and announced that he was going to retire, he found he had slipped from public grace. The people were now saying that he dared to fight only small bulls and that this new young Luis Miguel Dominguín was better and braver. Manolete had been on top too long. They wanted someone new.

Manolete had too much pride to quit under fire. He said he would have one last season, just a few short months, with the largest bulls in Spain, fighting with any fighters the promoters wished to bill him with. He wanted to retire untied and undefeated.

The next fights were not good. He wasn't up to it physically, and he wasn't helping himself by the way he was drinking. "They keep demanding more and more of me in every fight," he complained to me, "and I have no more to give." People want heroes, need heroes, but the Manolete myth had outgrown the real Manolete, and the people were angry at him for not living up to what they had created.

Then on August 28, 1947, he was to fight in Linares. It was extremely important to him that he be good this afternoon. First, it was near his hometown; second, Luis Miguel Dominguín was on the same program; and third, the bulls were Miuras, the famous "bulls of death," which have killed more great matadors than any other breed.

It began like any of his other fights—the stands were jammed with mantilla-draped señoritas and men with the broad-brimmed sombreros cocked over one eye; since it was midsummer and the sun shines till nine in Andalusia, the fight didn't start until six-thirty. Excitement filled the air because of the Miuras and the rivalry between Dominguín and Manolete.

The stylish gypsy Gitanillo de Triana completed the bill. Gitanillo did well by the first bull and received applause.

The second bull was Manolete's. It was dangerous and unpredictable, but Manolete was out to earn the award of an ear. He made the animal charge back and forth in front of him so closely and gracefully that even his detractors were up out of their seats and yelling. But when it came time to kill, he missed the first thrust. The second dropped the bull cleanly and the crowd applauded, but he had lost the ear; they were demanding perfection today.

The trumpet blew, and it was Luis Miguel's turn. This was an important fight for him also.

He strode out into the arena, good-looking, smug, twenty years old. Manolete was through—here was the new idol, here was the king of the rings!

He had the crowd roaring with the first fancy, twirling passes with the big cape. He put in his own banderillas superbly, to win more applause, and when he thrust the sword in between the withers up to the hilt, the animal sagged down dead, and the crowd cheered and waved their handkerchiefs until the president awarded him an ear.

Manolete had watched the entire performance from the passageway, with no change of expression. Those tricks and cape twirls were not his idea of true bullfighting. He would show the crowd what the real thing was if it killed him.

Gitanillo had a mediocre performance with his second animal. Then Manolete saw the toril gate swing open, and the last bull of his life, Islero, came skidding out of the tunnel. The moment Camará saw it hooking around the ring, he sucked in his breath and said to Manolete, "*Malo*—bad, bad. It hooks terribly to the right." That is a dread thing, for a matador must go over the right horn to kill. "Stay away from this one, *chico!*"

But Manolete was determined to give the best performance of his life. "Toro, hah, toroooo!" he called in his deep voice, holding the cape out in front of him and shaking it.

The animal wheeled at the voice, its tail shot up, and it charged across the ring. As it reached the cloth, the man did not spin or swirl the cape around him or dance about the way that Luis Miguel had done. He merely planted his feet and swung the cape slowly in front of the bull's nose, guiding the great head with the tantalizing cloth so that the left horn went by his legs ten inches away. Without moving his feet, he took the bull back in another charge, and the right horn stabbed the air six inches away from his thigh. Five more perfect, classic verónicas followed, each closer than the other, and he finished with a half-verónica that was so close that the bull's neck hit him and nearly knocked him off balance. He turned his back on the bewildered animal and looked up at the crowd, which was cheering deliriously.

With the muleta cape, his forte, he worked in even closer, until the crowd was shouting, "No, no!" Camará was shouting with them, for Manolete was passing the animal just as closely on the dangerous right side as on the left.

Finally, it was time to kill. As Manolete was lining up the Miura so that the feet would be together and the shoulder blades open, Camará and his banderilleros were yelling: "Stay away from him, man! Off to the side and get away quick!"

But Manolete had to finish this one right. He wasn't going to spoil the performance.

He stood in front of the Miura, sighting down the blade, rose on the toes of one foot, and as the bull lunged forward, Manolete hurled himself straight over the lowered right horn. The sword was sinking in when the bull wrenched its head to the right and drove the horn deep into the man's groin. Manolete was flung high into the air and slammed to the sand. The bull spiked at him twice on the ground, and then it staggered, choked, and flopped over dead.

In the ring infirmary, Manolete regained consciousness on the operating table. He gasped weakly, "Did it die?"

"*Si, chico, si,*" said Camará, tears raining down his cheeks. "It died and they didn't give me anything?" Manolete said, trying to raise himself from the table.

"They gave you everything, Matador," said a banderillero, putting his cigarette between the wounded man's lips. "Everything—both ears and tail."

He smiled and lay back.

An older banderillero, staring at the corpse, said dully, "They kept demanding more and more of him, and more was his life, so he gave it to them."

N iels, who managed the saloon, phoned me one morning. "Well, you sure blew it last night by not coming in. Orson Welles came into El Matador."

I was disappointed for there was no one I admired more and would have liked to have met. Damn—it seemed whenever I took a rare night off the most interesting people came in. A year later, in 1962, I met him in Spain. We were in the lobby of the Hotel Miramar in Malaga before the bullfight, and Herb Caen, who happened to be there, introduced me.

"I've read your books," Orson boomed.

"I've seen your films," I said.

"I have a little villa on the outskirts," he said. "Come for lunch tomorrow—come early and we'll talk about *los toros!*"

My wife and I went out to the villa in the late morning and sat out in the garden. Orson's wife, Paula, and his daughter, Rebecca, by Rita Hayworth, made appearances, but otherwise we were alone for several hours.

What an arresting figure he was, with his great head like a Rodin statue, his body like a Miura bull, and that magnificent voice. He dwarfed the lawn furniture; he made the garden appear smaller, this minotaur in his lair.

I was astonished by Orson's encyclopedic knowledge of bullfighting; this was one phase of the great man's versatility that had not been publicized.

"I studied bullfighting in Sevilla when I was seventeen and eighteen," he said, "and slim as Manolete I was! I fought several times professionally, but gave it up when I was gored badly."

I did not quite believe his story. Orson was given to, er, hyperbole. I guessed that he'd perhaps fought small cows at a few *tientas,* those events in the little rings on the ranches when the young animals are tested for bravery and spectators are allowed to try caping the females. Fighting cows is an activity not to be taken lightly, as many men have been gored (myself included) and even killed by them. But while I don't know if Orson Welles had ever fought a bull previously, I can tell you that he very definitely had an encounter with a bull before that day in Malaga was over.

I can also attest to the fact that he knew a lot about bullfighting, the lore, the toreros, and the techniques. He told me of a bullfighting film he'd shot but that, to his great disappointment, was never finished. "Greatest taurine footage ever!" He spoke of the amazing matadora, Conchita Cintrón, and of Juan Belmonte and Carlos Arruza and El Gallo. I tried to get him talking about his films, such as *Citizen Kane, The Magnificent Ambersons,* and *The Third Man,* but it was *la fiesta brava* that obsessed him. I did manage to change the subject once, briefly.

"Some time ago I heard a fine story about you," I said. "Apparently you were engaged to give a talk somewhere in the Midwest, and disappointed at the small crowd, you gazed around the room and started off: 'My name is Orson Welles—I'm an actor, producer, director, author, playwright, poet, mathematician, magician, and musician—isn't it a shame that there are so many of *me* and so few of *you!*'"

Orson chuckled.

"True story?" I asked.

"Happened in Des Moines," he said. "Now, getting back to Manolete . . . "

After a long lunch, we headed into Malaga for the afternoon corrida. At the *plaza de toros,* Orson, dressed in a black lumber jacket, immensed his way through the crowd, which parted in awe before him. At ringside he occupied two front-row seats. With us was the famed British critic Kenneth Tynan, who was filming the Malaga corridas. During the first fight, we exchanged opinions and argued about whether or not the bull's horns had been subjected to "shaving"—a shameful and increasingly prevalent practice in which the points of the horns are filed off to make the animals less dangerous. On the second bull, a strange thing happened: the matador, Palomo Linares, had killed his bull well, but when his assistant pulled the sword out of the dead animal, he carelessly flung it aside, it bounced, and the point somehow slashed the matador's calf. As they carried the bleeding man out to the infirmary, a friend of mine, a bull breeder named Pepe de la Cova, leaned forward and croaked in a stage whisper, "This is terrible—now we're going to have to start 'shaving' even the swords!"

Orson was still laughing at this when the trumpet blew for the third bull. The toril gate banged open directly across from us, and the huge black animal burst out. Then followed something that I've never seen in all my years of attending bullfights: the animal charged across the arena toward us, paying no attention to the bullfighter, speeding as though on rails straight at where we sat. When it came to the *barrera* fence, it didn't slow up but leapt unhesitatingly over the boards, its great bulk sailing up and over the *callejón* alleyway. As the crowd screamed, the animal landed with its front legs on either side of Orson's huge frame, perhaps targeted by his black jacket. Simultaneously, Orson jerked his body back and to the side, and the left horn slashed inches by his head. Orson froze, and for a split second, bull and man stared eye to eye. Then Orson and those of us around him shoved the bull, and it fell back on its side into the *callejón*. Unhurt, the animal scrambled to its feet and gored the first person it saw, the unfortunate ring carpenter. Finally, it was lured back into the arena, blood dripping from one horn.

Once the crowd recovered from the shock of the goring, and after the man had been rushed to the infirmary, they began to cheer Orson. I was amazed to see how completely calm he was; after all, the blood on that horn could very well have been his. He stood up and smiled and extended his arm, fingers closed, sweeping it slowly around the arena, like Manolete, like a triumphant matador. The crowd loved it.

It was an amazing incident. Luckily, the newspapers reported it the next day, and Tynan captured it on film, to satisfy any doubting *Tomás*. It was not the only time in history that a bull has managed to jump into the stands, but it is certainly the only time it has happened to an American, and a famous one at that.

The next day a reporter wrote in *La Prensa:*

"Why?" we asked the famous director in an exclusive interview, "why out of the 12,000 spectators in the arena did that wild bull of Cobaleda pick you to leap upon?"

Orson wagged his lion's head, great jowls a-quiver, and answered solemnly: "I have a deep affinity and empathy with bulls."

We then asked why he thought the bull chose to kill the hapless carpenter and not him, and the famous man answered simply: "One does not kill one's brother."

As I said, I'm not sure about Orson Welles' taurine career previous to that day in Malaga, but I can certainly bear witness to this one authentic encounter in a bullring.

"As far as I'm concerned," I told him over sherry later, "the next time you give a lecture you can add 'bullfighter' to that list of your many amazing achievements."

John Ireland and his then-wife, Joanne Dru, came into El Matador whenever they visited San Francisco.

Canadian-born but reared in New York's "Hell's Kitchen," John was the first professional actor I ever met. I was an undergraduate at Yale, he was in New Haven in *Macbeth* with Judith Anderson and Maurice Evans, and a friend brought him to lunch on the campus.

Aside from being an excellent and durable actor (he was nominated for an Oscar in *All The King's Men* and, most recently, played the lead in a remake of *Bonanza*), he was also an excellent tennis player and a merry luncheon companion. He was always catnip to the ladies and was legendary in Hollywood for his horizontal prowess.

"I still chase women," he joked not so long ago, "but I'm so grateful when they say no!"

Some years ago, *Esquire* magazine, in an in-depth article on that esoteric subject, listed him as one of the ten best-endowed men in the world. "Doesn't do me any good though," he said. "You see, when I get excited, the blood rushes from my head and I faint."

In film circles, there is a story about his endowment which three different people have told me. It goes like this: John and his agent were leaving an athletic club locker room after a workout. A husky young man emerged from the steam room wrapped in a towel.

"Hey, Ireland," he challenged, "I've heard about you! I'll bet one hundred dollars mine's bigger!"

John continued walking, saying, "Yeah? Hooray for you."

The other man pursued him. "Two hundred! What's the matter—afraid?"

"Get lost, buster," Ireland said, trying to ignore him.

"Three hundred!" said the other.

At this point, the agent stopped and said with a resigned sigh, "Come on, John, just take out enough to win the bet."

I always wondered if this were an authentic story, and one day in the Matador I let my curiosity overcome the indelicacy of the question; I retold the vulgar story to John and asked if it were true.

John looked shocked. "*Good heavens!*" Then he glanced around him, and said craftily, "You got three hundred on you?"

While many famous people came into the Matador over the years, 90 percent of "Our Dear Regulars," as my manager Niels called them, were not famous at all, of course. One of the most faithful was Dickie Kraemer, who didn't drink but loved what he called "the artistic atmosphere of the Mat."

A Jewish friend of mine once said, "Dickie is not a schlemiel, as is commonly supposed; he is a schlemozzle."

I dutifully asked what the difference was.

"A schlemiel is the kind of guy who goes to a fancy party and during dinner, tips over the soup tureen. That's a schlemiel. It *spills* on the schlemozzle. Dickie, for better or worse, is a schlemozzle."

Of this middle-aged eccentric, an old classmate of his said once, "I love Dickie, but, of course, he's one taco shy of the combination plate. His wife, whom he married in his teens, died just after they graduated from Stanford, and he's never been the same since." A multimillionaire ("my uncle invented stop lights . . . "), he dressed terribly, drove a battered old Chevy, and spent most of his money on zoos and animal causes. I never met anyone who truly loved animals so much. He loved all four-legged creatures, but his specialty was orphaned foxes. He was a fox nut. He owned red foxes, gray foxes, arctic foxes, desert foxes, and kit foxes. People only visited his apartment once, no matter how fond they were of the lovable little guy. The smell.

For twenty years, he kept his beloved Chinese pheasant, Phezzy, perched on the end of his bed. Below the bird, who never moved off the bedstead, there arose a remarkable lime stalagmite. With all those foxes around, Phezzy was a very neurotic bird. And with reason.

"One day last week the maid left the bedroom door open," Dickie told me once in his adenoidal voice. "And Sweetheart, the gray, got in. Oh my, oh my, I got home just in time! That room looked like a snowstorm had hit it—it looked as though someone had busted a pillow wide open! Terrible!"

But Dickie gave the limp, denuded bird mouth-to-beak resuscitation and rushed it to a vet. Phezzy somehow survived and continued to live on the end of the bed.

Dickie's largesse to the San Francisco Zoo and his love of animals never abated, even after, while attending a rally for owners of wild pets, a hyena bit him in the genitals and put him in the hospital for three weeks. Dickie was the kind of person rarely referred to without the word "poor" in front of his name: "Heard about poor Dickie? Got his balls nearly bit off by a hyena yesterday!" Yet everyone liked him.

Next to animals, Dickie's great passion was writing song lyrics. He wrote constantly and passionately, and he was unquestionably the worst writer I have ever encountered. One day he told me he had finished his masterpiece, a serious musical based on *Wuthering Heights*, book and lyrics by Richard Kraemer. He gave me the huge tome to read. In the first scene, Cathy Earnshaw "strolls out on the moors and sings plaintively. . . . ":

> I would give my eye-teeth if
> I could see Heathcliff . . .

It went downhill from there. In a Kingsley Amis novel, one character says about another's terrible poems, "Put it this way, if they were ballet dancers, you'd have to cover up your eyes until you were quite sure they'd all finished and gone off."

But he was never discouraged by a lifetime of rejections, and he kept writing. A great event in his life was when Arthur Fiedler, the conductor, came into the Matador, topped only by the times Hoagy Carmichael and Noel Coward paid their visits.

He would hire well-known composers to write music to his lyrics, pay a Hollywood orchestra to record them, and then pass the records around to his friends in the Matador.

I remember another memorable line from a later opus, a musical drama based on the life of Catherine the Great:

> When I take you out for Easter
> I'll kiss you on your keester.

In vain did I try to convince him that "keester" was not a synonym for "face."

Dickie's most memorable lines were not lyrics, and even in the face of death he maintained his characteristic cheerfulness. He called me one day to say he had developed lung cancer. "Gosh," he said, "I thought it only happened to others, to one's Aunt Clara." Nothing in his life became Dickie like his leaving it. He was extremely brave. Two days before he died in his bed, with Phezzy still perched on the end, he called me.

"I don't mind dying so much," he said, "but I didn't think I'd feel so sick." His last words to me were, "Promise me you won't forget to help the animals. . . . "

Some years before he died, Dickie gave my family a pet we will forever remember. One day, he left off at the Matador a parakeet cage, and attached to it was a note that read: "Zorro is an orphan, a five-week-old, tree-climbing gray fox—and I know you'll love him. Feed bitch's milk (at any vet's) every couple of hours."

In the cage was a reddish-gray ball of fluff, not much bigger than my fist, with a little bushy tail. For a moment, one might have thought it was a kitten, except for those ears—big, like on Egyptian statues of felines—and those oriental eyes—chartreuse around moist black olives—and that pointy black nose. No cat he!

I put my hand into the cage, and the little creature, completely unafraid, licked my fingers and whined hungrily. When I got home, my wife, Mary, gently lifted the fox out of his cage, put him on the kitchen table, and fed him with an eye dropper, while Michael, my ten-year-old stepson, and I watched. Every family has an "animal child" and Michael was ours. Our pets also took to the newcomer immediately: Samantha, the haughtiest of Himalayan-Siamese cats, cleaned the little fox thoroughly, and Tomás, the bouncy pug puppy, fetched his precious rubber ball and placed it in front of the stranger in an offer to play. The little fox wobbled forward, touched noses with the dog, and they were pals for life.

Over the next year, the unlikely friendship grew among the three animals as Zorro developed into a gray, white, and russet beauty with a magnificent brush. He was totally tame and loving and immaculately clean and odorless. Zorro was housebroken immediately, newspaper trained, though sometimes, alas, when one was reading it. He had a fine vulpine sense of humor: Zorro would toy with the slow and slightly dim-witted dog as they charged through the kitchen and around the living room. During these hot pursuits, the nimble fox would slow up for the puffing little fatso, brush his full tail across the dog's eyes to confuse him, and then leap gracefully to a bureau or the mantle and gaze down at his frustrated pursuer, a smile actually curling the corners of his mouth.

Samantha was far too regal to engage in such antics, but she loved Zorro and would deign to curl up and sleep with him from time to time.

Our children adored him and he them, and when one day he somehow slipped out of the back yard and didn't come back, they were heartbroken. Zorro had set out on little forays before, but neighbors had always called to say they'd seen him, and we'd either gone to pick him up or he'd returned home on his own, scratching at the door to be let in.

But this time he didn't come home, and no one telephoned. When several days went by and still no Zorro at the door, no foxes reported in the pound, and no answer to our classified ad, I started to give up. At the end of the week, I sat the children down and gave them a solemn consolation talk, which really amounted to half-hearted rationalizations. But Michael, our animal child, wouldn't accept this; he refused to give up.

Every day after school, Michael would ride his bike to nearby Washington Park and spend hours calling, "Zorry, here Zorry!" He phoned the pound regularly, scanned the lost and found columns every day, and stopped strangers on the street to ask if they'd seen a fox. They'd shake their heads and look at him strangely: A fox? In San Francisco?

I phoned Herb Caen, asked for help, and Herb ran not one but two items in his column on the lost pet.

Two weeks went by, and we had only two false leads to show for our efforts. Still, Michael would not give up. He called Carter B. Smith, a popular disk jockey, who aired the human interest story three times on station KSFO.

On the seventeenth day after the fox's disappearance, the phone rang and a rough male voice said, "This is the superintendent of the cable car barn on Washington

Street. We got a gray varmint down here—could be that fox I heard about on the radio. He's got a collar on but we can't catch him."

Luckily, it was a Saturday, so I grabbed Michael, we jumped into the car, and sped down to the cable car barn, praying that it wasn't another false alarm. We raced into the courtyard of the brick structure where the cable cars are stored at night.

"He's been coming up for our sandwiches outta there," said the superintendent, pointing to a large opening at the end of the cable slot. "But he's too fast for us to catch."

Michael cupped his hands and shouted, "Zorry!"

In a moment, a pointed nose appeared out of the hole, then the entire, beautiful gray body.

"Zorry!" Michael called again.

And to the amazement of the superintendent and several workers, the fox streaked across the courtyard toward us and leapt into Michael's arms. There were tears in my eyes, and the men cheered as the boy hugged his pet.

All the way home Zorro whined with joy and licked our faces. He was painfully thin. How had he managed to live for seventeen days? Had he stolen crabs from Fisherman's Wharf, dried ducks from Chinatown markets, or pizza scraps from North Beach garbage pails?

Most moving of all was when we arrived at the house and Zorro met Mary, whom the fox loved best. After a joyous reunion with the cat and the pug, Zorro flopped over on his side. Then he pulled himself along the entire length of the carpet toward Mary, crooning softly, his head thrown back, the jugular exposed, totally vulnerable, the ultimate expression of submission and devotion in the fox world.

And we were a family again.

Mary Pickford came into the Matador one night. Yes, the legend. Infirm and alcoholic, the old silent screenstar had been retired for decades and rarely traveled anywhere. So I was amazed when Pickford, "America's Sweetheart," appeared in my saloon, pushed in a wheelchair by her younger husband, "America's Boyfriend," Buddy Rogers. She told me she'd come up from Los Angeles to see Maurice Chevalier perform. She said, "You know, Maurice told me yesterday that he couldn't come to lunch, that he stays in bed all day right up to show time just so he'll be able to give a good performance! Imagine at his age taking show business that seriously. Why, I told Maurice, you silly goose, you're over eighty, you just quit this nonsense right this minute and retire!"

I, for one, am glad he didn't take Mary's advice, for the next night I saw the show. It was a nonstop, two-hour, one-man performance—no chimpanzee act or stand-up comic to fill it out—just a sleek, gray-haired Maurice Chevalier, in tuxedo, straw boater, white scarf, and cane, and a lively orchestra in the pit. He sang every one of his famous songs, from "Gigi" to "Mimi" to "Valentine" (*vah-lawn-teen-uh*). He sang French music hall ballads, a handful I'd never heard before plus ones I remembered from when I was about ten, like "Yew Brawt A Noo Kant Off Lawf To Me." He told stories about his loves—Mistinguette, Josephine Baker, and Marlene Dietrich—and included droll introductions to several songs. He even did amusing little dance steps between choruses.

It's impossible to describe the man's charm and vitality, his energy! This was the greatest single performance I've ever seen on the stage. The audience went wild and insisted on six encores, which he gave us delightedly. It seemed he never wanted to leave the stage, and we certainly didn't want him to. His last song was his famous hit, "Every leetle breeze seems to wheesper Louise," which left the audience with tears of joy and nostalgia.

The next day I was invited to a reception for Chevalier at the Fairmont Hotel given by financier Louis Lurie. He and Maurice were old friends and often celebrated their same birthday, September 12, 1888, together. Maurice chatted with everyone, radiating joy, just as electric in person as he'd been on the stage. I confronted him with Mary Pickford's accusation that he never got out of bed all day. He chuckled, put his arm around Lurie, and said, "For Mahree Peek-for' I don' get out of bed. For mon cher Louis Lurie, for thees wonnerfool fren', I get out of bed!" (Chevalier made his first movie in Hollywood in 1928, yet his French accent seemed to grow stronger with each passing year.)

Later at the party, as the huge cake was being cut, a reporter asked Maurice how it felt to be eighty, and his answer has been quoted many, many times: "Considering the alternative," he said with that inimitable smile, "not too bad, not too bad at all."

Then the smile faded and he added, "Seriously, after eighty every man should have hees suitcase packed."

I was lucky to have seen that performance, for it turned out to be one of his last. A month later, on October 20, he appeared to have taken Mary Pickford's advice: he announced his retirement after sixty-eight years in show business. He retreated to his big home in Marnes La Coquette near Paris.

But without the footlights he thrived on, he seemed to wither and shrink. Occasionally, he would go out to dine with the Duke and Duchess of Windsor or some other old friend. But he soon fell into a deep depression and retreated from all society. He died on New Year's Day 1972.

"I should have stayed on the stage," he said gloomily, just before his death at eighty-four, "and died on it."

During the many years of his career, Gary Cooper, perhaps more than any other actor in motion pictures, became the symbol for the American male here and abroad. Between 1926 and his death in 1961, he appeared in ninety-two feature films, over and over proving himself to be brave but sensitive, bold but shy, tough but fair, a ladies' man certainly but first and foremost a man's man. He made millions of boys want to lead a wagon train and just as many girls want to kiss a sheriff.

The actor Anthony Perkins, who appeared with Cooper in *Friendly Persuasion*, summed him up nicely: "When Gary walked on a set, the technicians stopped. The hammers stopped hammering, not because he demanded it, but in tribute. Cooper was the model for a gentleman actor, for the star—the modesty of behavior, the elegance of carriage, the aristocratic bearing."

I'm not sure who brought Gary into El Matador or even what he was doing in San Francisco in 1957. But it was easy to strike up a friendship with him: we had Montana in common.

Gary was born in Helena, Montana, and his father, Frank Cooper, was the bailiff in the court that my grandfather, Judge William Henry Hunt, presided over. Frank Cooper eventually became a judge himself. My uncle, also named William Hunt, was a friend of Gary's; he left Yale to go to Hollywood and become a stunt man and bit player in Gary's films.

"I'm going to be in Mexico next month," Gary said, as he left the nightclub. "Sure would like to go to a bullfight with you."

As it happened, I was doing a book on the matador Carlos Arruza, and so I rendezvoused in Mexico City with Gary and his current *inamorata,* the stunning half-Mexican, half-Swedish model, Lorraine Chanel. Gary was even better looking offscreen, and the big surprise was that, unlike his monosyllabic screen image—"Yup, nope,

much obliged, ma'am"—he turned out to be voluble, ar-
ticulate, and extremely well informed on a variety of subjects. He wanted to go to the bullfights with me to learn
more about "that fascinating sport."

The year before, he'd been in Spain, had gone out to a
tienta, where the young animals are tested, and found
himself in the little arena with a two-year-old animal.

"I've been around dangerous livestock all my life, cattle, broncs, brahma bulls, but I've never known such pure
fear as I felt in that arena, walking out with nothing but a
cape toward that horned animal. A few moments before
in the corral, it had looked so small and tubercular and
now looked like a Greyhound bus. I took an awful beat-
ing, but I also managed to do a couple of adequate passes
and got some olé's, and that was better than any Hollywood applause that I ever received."

We went to the real bullfights the next day, and as we
made our way to the stands, several urchins crowded
around Cooper, patting him on the back and chest and
chanting delightedly, "Gah-ree! Gah-ree!"

"Gosh," said the actor, dipping his head modestly.
"These young fans sure are nice. I didn't know I had such
a following down here." Then the adulators disappeared,
suddenly, and it wasn't until we got in our seats that Gary
discovered that his "fans" had got his money clip out of
his pants pocket, his watch off his wrist, his wallet out of
the breast pocket of his jacket, and his passport out of the
side pocket.

"Well, I'll be a monkey's uncle," said the chagrined but
resigned victim, sounding very much like the onscreen
Gary Cooper.

The whole world was sad when it learned in 1961 that
Gary had terminal cancer. At the Oscar ceremony that
year, director William Wyler announced an Honorary
Award for him, calling him "the kind of American who's
loved in the four corners of the earth."

As Coop lay dying, Ernest Hemingway, who was also facing death, called his old friend.

"I'll bet," Coop told the author, with no self-pity, "I make it to the barn before you do."

He died shortly after that, six days after his sixtieth birthday. He won the bet.

As one might guess, El Matador attracted anyone who was interested in *la fiesta brava*. The huge mounted bull's head behind the bar, Juan Belmonte's suit of lights hanging on the wall, the life-size portrait of Manolete, the dozens of photos of the immortals, and the huge mural of the Sevilla arena all made the aficionados feel at home. And several actual bullfighters or their families came in.

One evening, a short, dapper Spaniard was introduced to me as "the nephew of Blanquet." Had I heard of Blanquet? Of course, everyone in bullfighting had heard his story.

Hemingway said that Blanquet "could smell impending death" and that he did so on three celebrated occasions. "Was it true?" I asked the quiet graying man, his nephew. He nodded, and over several sherries told me this extraordinary tale, which at first I didn't believe; it was too much like a yarn by Guy de Maupassant. But since then I have researched it in Spain and talked to people who had actually witnessed the events, and it's all true.

Enrique Belenguer, called Blanquet, was not much to look at, but he is considered one of the finest banderilleros of all time; while never a star himself, a good banderillero is a vital part of a matador's team, protecting his matador, saving his life if he gets knocked down by a bull, and, in general, trying to help him during the fight. Blanquet almost never made a false move in the arena, and he never made a bad guess.

"He was a very small man," Hemingway wrote, "very serious and honorable with a Roman nose and an almost grey face, who had the greatest intelligence of the bull-fight I have ever seen and a cape that seemed magic in correcting the faults of the bull. . . . "

Blanquet's greatest talent was making the matadors he worked for look good, and his services were always in demand. In 1914, he became the number one banderillero for Joselito, generally acknowledged to be the finest all-around matador in history. For six years, Blanquet served his master faithfully and saved his life innumerable times. Unbelievably, the "Invincible" Joselito was never injured seriously. Then came May 16, 1920, and the fateful corrida in Talavera de la Reina where Joselito was to perform with his brother-in-law, Ignacio Sánchez Mejías.

As they lined up to make the parade into the arena, Blanquet said that he smelled candles burning. "Can't you smell it?" he asked Sánchez Mejías. "The last time I smelled it so strongly was at my father's funeral. I don't feel right about today."

Joselito laughed at him and clapped him on the shoulder.

Joselito had trouble killing his first bull. His second, Bailador, was very small—but it was a full five years old, and age is always a more dangerous factor than size in a bull. Joselito immediately recognized the treacherous charge of the animal, but toward the end of the encounter he let down his guard for a moment. The bull attacked, ripped open the man's stomach, and Joselito died a few moments later in the infirmary.

Blanquet was crushed by the death of his idol and master, and he did not fight for over a year. Then there appeared on the scene the greatest torero since Joselito: a nineteen-year-old Valencian, Manuel Granero.

"We need you," Granero's manager begged Blanquet. "Besides, he's from your hometown."

Blanquet served Granero as faithfully and well as he had served Joselito—and the handsome young Valencian was soon the most popular torero in Spain. Then came the corrida of May 7, 1922, in Madrid. As they stood at the gate waiting for the trumpet to signal the start of the parade, Blanquet went pale.

"Something terrible is happening," he cried out. "I smell candle wax very strongly—the last time I smelled it was two years ago. Just like this. It was the day that Joselito was killed." And again it happened; Pocapena, the fifth bull of that afternoon, snagged Granero by the leg, slammed him against the fence, and drove a horn into his brain.

After Granero's death, there was much talk about Blanquet's premonitory words. Some of the toreros even made uneasy café jokes that a matador would always be safe with Blanquet and "his warning system" around. But Blanquet swore that he would never again enter a bullring. He sold his "suit of lights" and went into business in Valencia.

Several years later, however, Joselito's brother-in-law, Matador Sánchez Mejías, went to see him. "I'm getting on," he said. "I can't take chances now with anyone but the best to help me."

Blanquet refused at first, but business had not been good, and finally he agreed. Once back in harness, he was the same old Blanquet. Although forty-five years old, the veteran banderillero was as agile as a man of thirty, but his bravery and knowledge of bulls were even more valuable than his athletic ability.

On Sunday, August 15, 1926, an important fight was booked in Sevilla, the most bull-wise city in the bullfighting world. The bullfighters lined up at the arena gate and looked across the golden sand at the packed stands, waiting for the parade.

Suddenly, Blanquet went pale and began to tremble. "Oh God, not again," he whispered.

Another banderillero, who had witnessed both Joselito's and Granero's deaths, asked with alarm, "The smell of funeral candles?"

Blanquet leaned against the gatepost and nodded. The word ran quickly among the other bullfighters. Only Sánchez Mejías, a very brave torero, seemed to take it lightly.

"Of course you smell candles," he joked. "Look how close by the cathedral is."

Nevertheless, it turned out to be one of the worst bullfight programs in Sevilla's season. All of the nervous toreros worked as far away from the bulls' horns as possible. And when Sánchez Mejías finally killed the last bull of the afternoon, all the bullfighters breathed easier. They even joked about it as they hurried to catch the train for Madrid, still dressed in their costumes.

As they stepped into their train compartment, Blanquet said apologetically, "I'm a superstitious old fool. I shouldn't have worried everyone." But still he looked perplexed. "Why was I wrong this time?"

Sánchez Mejías took out a bottle of wine. "Have a drink and forget it, *compadre*."

Blanquet started to take off his jacket. Abruptly, he gasped, clutched his chest, and pitched forward to the floor. They rushed the veteran banderillero to the hospital, where he was pronounced dead of a heart attack.

So, many years later in the Matador, his nephew finished his glass of sherry and said, "People said that my uncle seemed to go with a strange wisdom, a knowledge and familiarity with death that only he knew about. He died with a smile on his lips—he'd been right every time."

In the years between his fourth book, *Tobacco Road* in 1933, and his fifty-fifth book, *With All My Might* in 1987, the year of his death, Erskine Caldwell established himself as the most widely read living writer in the world. Some 80 million copies of his books in forty-odd languages have been sold. Faulkner once named him as "one of the five best contemporary writers."

I saw a lot of "Skinny" and his wife, Virginia, in the fifties and sixties, nearly always in El Matador; he was an enthusiastic customer. To meet him you might think he was born a courtly plantation owner from Virginia. In reality, his father was a Presbyterian minister from Georgia whose salary had been $350 a year. His mother was a teacher who made his clothes and taught him at home. As a child, his very best friend was a black boy named Bisco (about whom he wrote a book, *In Search of Bisco*).

Dirt poor all his early life, Caldwell was twenty-five years old when renowned editor Maxwell Perkins offered to buy two of his short stories. When the excited Caldwell, who could hardly believe it, asked what he would be paid, Perkins answered, "Two-fifty for both."

"Two-fifty?" Caldwell said. "I don't know. I thought I'd receive a little more than that." Perkins upped the offer to three-fifty. "I guess that would be okay," said Caldwell. "But I sort of thought I'd get more than three and a half dollars for both of them." "Oh, no!" Perkins said. "I meant three hundred and fifty dollars."

Erskine Caldwell was never broke again. *Tobacco Road* was a huge and controversial success; then he wrote *God's Little Acre* and had a lucrative stint in Hollywood as a screenwriter. The capper was the Broadway version of *Tobacco Road*, which played for seven and a half years, broke all attendance records, and brought Caldwell two thousand a week.

Hard-drinking, hard-working, taciturn, he was a gentle man, thoughtful and friendly, but hard to know. The loudest I ever heard him laugh was one night at a cocktail party at famed attorney Mel Belli's colorful Barbary Coast law offices in San Francisco: Mel introduced Niven Busch, the best-selling novelist (*Duel In the Sun*), to Caldwell.

"Do you two know each other?" Belli asked.

"No," said Busch, extending his hand, "but last week my ex- wife played your ex-wife on TV."

It was true: the actress Teresa Wright had played the part of Margaret Bourke-White, the great photographer, in a television documentary about her battle with Parkinson's disease.

Skinny laughed loud and long, and later in El Matador he repeated the story about his ex-wife to anyone who would listen.

It was 1988, and I was driving out of the little town of Carpinteria, California, toward my home on the beach when I saw a figure hitchhiking along the freeway. He looked familiar, almost like the political gadfly Dick Tuck. Sure enough, it was Dick Tuck. I stopped, picked him up, and took him back to my house for lunch.

Almost forgotten now, this white-haired leprechaun was Richard Nixon's nemesis, among other things. I'd met him many years ago when he virtually lived at El Matador, conspiring with famed journalist Pierre Salinger and the like. He was a famous political figure in his day, but explaining exactly what he did in politics is pretty tough. To say he pulled dirty tricks and was a Nixon-baiter and political prankster par excellence hardly does the job. Examples must be given. Here's his account of one of his most famous pranks, which took place during Richard Nixon's 1962 campaign for governor of California.

"So, I was working for Pat Brown, who was the governor and up for reelection," Tuck said. "So we're in L.A., and we hear that Dick Nixon, our opponent, is doing a thing in Chinatown. I decide maybe we can smoke Nixon out on the $205,000 unsecured loan that Howard Hughes gave to his brother, Don.

"I get to his event, and I make up a big sign that says, in Chinese characters, 'How about the Hughes loan?' Above that I write 'Welcome Nixon' in English. There's one TV news crew there, and I tip them off that Nixon may be about to do something interesting. So Nixon's standing there posing with this kid holding up my sign when a Chinese elder suddenly says, 'No, no, no.'

"Nixon says, 'What do you mean, 'No, no, no?'

"When the man explains what the Chinese characters say, Nixon grabs the sign out of the kid's hand and tears it up. Right there on camera."

His prank on Nixon in Chinatown made him a legend in American politics, but he said that he nearly topped it later in that 1962 campaign. While Nixon was speaking on the back of a train in San Luis Obispo, Tuck donned a conductor's uniform and waved the train out of the station.

"Nixon's up there talking, and suddenly the crowd goes out like the morning tide," said Tuck, chuckling.

Later Tuck became a close aide to Senator Robert F. Kennedy, who liked his wit, not to mention his interest in tormenting Nixon. With Nixon the likely Republican nominee for president in 1968, Kennedy wanted Tuck around as he headed for the Democratic nomination.

Then Kennedy was assassinated on the night he won the California primary. Tuck was with the senator when Kennedy made his fateful walk through the kitchen of the Ambassador Hotel. While others screamed and lunged for the gunman, Sirhan B. Sirhan, Tuck took off his suit jacket and gently placed it under the head of the dying Kennedy.

"For me, for a long time, all the joy was gone from politics after Bobby was killed," Tuck said.

Before he left my house that day, he told me one story that is delightful, nonpolitical, but totally Tuckian.

In San Francisco, an influential female friend offered to let him stay in her elegant Pacific Heights house completely free while she went to Europe for two months. She only asked that Dick take wonderful care of Hermione, her precious cat.

Everything went swimmingly between Dick and Hermione—lots of catnip and tuna and combing—until the day before the woman was due home, when disaster struck: while backing out of the driveway, Dick ran over and killed the cat.

Horrified, he put Hermione in a shoe box and sped downtown. At Robison's famous pet shop in Maiden Lane, Dick plunked the box on the counter, took the lid off, and said to the clerk: "Match that cat!"

Among the dozens of felines in the store, there was one that resembled Hermione closely, but it was a male. Frantically, Dick made the rounds of several other pet shops in San Francisco with no luck. Time was running out. Then he remembered the city pound and hurried there.

"Can you match that cat?" he asked.

Miraculously, they could. The new Hermione was almost an exact copy and was soon installed back in the Pacific Heights house. The next day, Dick awaited his friend's return with great trepidation. The first encounter went smoothly.

"My, how you've grown, Hermione!" was all that she said. Dick sighed with relief and departed, his relationship with the woman intact.

And that would have been the end of the matter, had Hermione not given birth to two kittens the following week. The woman had had the real Hermione spayed a few months before, and when she threatened to sue the veterinarian who had done the operation, Dick Tuck, always an enemy of injustice, felt he had to confess all.

"And thus I lost another important connection," Dick sighed as we drove. I deposited his elfin figure on the edge of the freeway so that he could continue his journey to Malibu.

I never did ask why he was hitchhiking or what he was up to. Damn. It was probably a good story, too.

For a short time, Lucille Ball was the host of a radio talk show. I guess she had run out of interviewees in Los Angeles because she came to San Francisco to interview "colorful characters in their own environment." I suggested the Mat but when her producer made an appointment for Lucille to visit with me, it was not at the club but at our Victorian house on Octavia Street. Our young kids went slightly crazy.

"You mean 'I Love Lucy' herself is coming *here?*"

I gave them a little admonitory lecture the night before The Big Day.

"Look, I've never met Miss Ball, but remember that those 'I Love Lucy' programs you love so much were made many, *many* years ago. She's probably changed a whole lot, so prepare yourself for her not being exactly the same."

"Oh, sure," they said. "We realize *that.*"

Each of the kids wanted to be the one selected to open the door for Miss Ball, but Billy, aged ten and our serious actor, was elected by drawing straws.

We were all waiting in the living room when the big moment finally arrived, the doorbell ringing precisely at noon. Billy jumped up like a shot, perspiring in his excitement. As he and I hurried toward the door, I whispered, "Now remember, she might look different, but of course don't comment on it! Don't say that she looks different."

"Of course," said Billy loftily. "Think I'm dumb?"

He took a deep breath and flung open the door.

Standing there in person, tall in spike heels, tape recorder in her white-gloved hands, chauffeur behind her, was the star of film, television, and radio, Lucille Ball. She was a startling sight. Her shock of incendiary hair was a wild orange conflagration, her eyelids were a shiny kodachrome blue, her false eyelashes an inch long, her lips were a great scarlet slash, and she was wearing a fur coat the color of an orangutan.

"Geez!" Billy cried out, recoiling a step. "Geez, you look different!"

"Oh?" said Miss Ball coolly. "You mean, I look older, little boy?"

Billy recovered wonderfully. He only gulped once before saying, "Oh, no, Miss Ball. You, you just—just look so much better than you do on TV."

Miss Ball smiled and patted him on his head.

"You'll go far," she said as she stepped into the house, "you lying little bastard."

That night in El Matador, my editor, John Dodds, who married Vivian Vance, Lucy's sidekick Ethel Mertz on "I Love Lucy," told me of the night Lucille Ball and Ethel Merman were drinking by themselves, hard and late, in Sardi's Broadway restaurant. Producer Billy Rose sat down with them and replaced their empty champagne bottle with a full one. Lucille noticed Billy's cuff links, tiny, silver derringer pistols.

"They really work," said Billy, taking one off and handing it to Lucille. "They fire a little cap."

Ethel Merman was wearing a very low dress; Lucille cocked the pistol, closed one eye, and took wobbly aim at Ethel's chest.

"Fire when ready, Gridley ol' girl," said Ethel, "ol' girl, ol' girl!"

Lucille pulled the trigger, the pistol made a little bang, and a tiny burning wad flew out and stuck on Ethel's left breast. Ethel jumped up screaming, and Vince Sardi hurried over, a wet napkin at the ready. He put out the spark, and the moaning victim was helped to the ladies room for repairs and a Band-Aid.

John Dodds happened by the table at that point and saw Lucille sitting there, downing more champagne, choking back sobs, her tears ruining her mascara.

"What's the matter, Lucy?" asked John. "Why are you crying?"

"You'd cry, too," said Lucille with a little sob, "if you'd just shot your best friend in the tit with a cuff link!"

I met Dr. Luis Jiménez-Guinea, the greatest horn-wound specialist in the world, the hard way.

The whole thing started in 1958 when two old friends showed up at the Matador one night and invited me to come to Spain with them the next week, all expenses paid, if I'd "show them the bullfighting world."

One can take just so much of nightclub life day after day and the chance to revisit old haunts was irresistible, so I left Niels in charge of El Matador and flew off to Spain with John and Diana Redington. On our third day in Madrid, an aristocratic Spaniard of my acquaintance approached me in the lobby of the Palace Hotel.

"There's an international bullfight being held for charity day after tomorrow," said the genial hidalgo. "There's a Frenchman, a Mexican, and a Spaniard, and—to represent America—we want you!"

My stomach muscles constricted. The very thought of fighting a bull at this point in my life was like expecting an elevator to go up when it suddenly goes down. I was thirty-six, way over the hill in taurine terms. After all, the great Manolete came out of retirement at thirty, got himself gored by a Miura bull, and even the skills of the famed Dr. Luis Jiménez-Guinea failed to save him.

Why didn't I just say, "Hey, I'm rusty, I'm old, I haven't fought for years, I'm a married man with kids—get someone else"? It would have been so easy. The eighteenth century writer, Thomas Fuller, once said that "many would be cowards if they had but courage enough," and since I didn't have courage enough to say no, I heard myself saying yes to this potentially lethal invitation.

When I found myself actually dressed in fighting costume and waiting outside the small arena in El Escorial near Madrid and heard the roar of the excited crowd, the pounding of my heart sounded like a kettledrum. I remembered my teacher, the great, fearless matador Juan Belmonte, had said once, "If we had to sign the contracts on the day of the fight itself, there would be no bullfights."

If there had been an honorable way to get out of the fight, I would have. But now, of course, it was too late; the march into the ring had begun. I saw the Redingtons in the front row looking apprehensive.

Claude Popelin, the distinguished French author and amateur matador, was to perform first. His bull was let into the arena, and it came in with a fierce rush, charging wildly at the first cape it saw. This animal had never been tormented, yet it knew why it was in the ring. The man might have been an amateur, but the animal was a professional.

These creatures have been raised for centuries for one purpose only, to try to kill men. They are a separate breed from their domestic cousin, a wild animal as different in looks and temperament as a German shepherd is from a wolf. The *toro bravo* is the most perfect living instrument for killing that man has been able to create by selective breeding, over hundreds of years. *Bred*, not taught, to fight, a month-old calf will attack. They are not trained to charge any more than a rattlesnake needs to be trained to strike. In all their four or five years, they do not encounter a dismounted man until the day of their fight, and they fight only once. If they are selected to go to the arena, they live twice as long as if they are condemned to McDonald's. Perhaps the only creature on earth that, when aroused, has no consideration for its own preservation, a fighting bull will unhesitatingly charge an automobile or a train.

And what of the men who must face these fierce and lethal creatures? Are they afraid? As afraid as I was that afternoon?

The answer is a resounding yes. How could they help but be when the statistics are reviewed? Most top bullfighters expect to be gored, with varying severity, at least once a season, and several aspirant toreros are killed in Spain and South America each year. Nine star matadors have been killed in the arena since the great Manolete's death in 1947, one famous veteran by a calf in a practice ring on a ranch. That animal had been much smaller than the one Claude Popelin was about to confront. Would he be up to it? I saw him yawn, a sure sign of fear. But then he bravely stepped out with the animal, the big cape held in front of him. The animal charged, and he led it by his body several times, guiding the deadly horns only inches away from his legs by the skillful manipulation of the cloth. Fear was nowhere in evidence, and the crowd cheered wildly again and again. Here they were seeing Hemingway's "grace under pressure."

Nowhere in the modern world is the difference between cowardice and courage more clearly defined and more on display than in the *plaza de toros*. The audience, "the only beast in the arena," as Blasco Ibáñez observed in *Blood and Sand*, goes to the bullring for one purpose— to see men behave differently from the way *they* would behave if they were down there in the arena facing half a ton of wild animal with horns like sabers.

Finally, it was my turn. My animal was smaller, but its horns were larger, and sharper. It raced around the empty arena, hooking into the boards of the red barrier. As I watched, I can honestly say that the fear I felt was not so much the dry-mouthed fear of being wounded or killed but simply the fear of making a fool of myself in front of all these people, of being exposed as inept or, worse, a coward.

I grabbed my cape and went out determined to outdo the other matadors. I made a good pass and the crowd cheered, but I noticed that the animal hooked dangerously with its right horn. On the next pass, I slid my feet back a few inches out of the path of the stilleto point.

I did several more passes to applause. And then it happened. In the middle of guiding the horns past my legs, the animal swerved violently to the right. I was impaled on the horn and raised into the air as the crowd screamed. The horn sliced into my inner left leg and spiked nine inches through the muscle. I somehow got off the horn and came down on my feet. Another bullfighter distracted the animal, flashing a cape in its face, and I lurched to the fence.

I didn't know I'd been gored. It had simply felt like a hard punch from a fist. I saw the Redingtons in the audience pointing, and I looked down. I had one red shoe and one black one. The blood was pumping down my leg like water out of a garden hose.

An hour later I was in the Madrid hospital, where I met Dr. Jiménez-Guinea, the great horn-wound specialist. A large man, he looked like an angry General Douglas MacArthur. As I was being wheeled into the emergency room, the doctor examined the wound and said in his hoarse, matter-of-fact voice, "Just like Manolete's goring."

This was not encouraging.

A day later, as I lay critically ill, he said with his usual subtle bedside manner, "You are very bad off. Are you married?"

I nodded weakly.

"Tell her to come—*dile que venga!*"

"She's in California," I gasped. "It will take two days to get here."

"*Dile que no venga!*" he said. "You'll either be well or dead by then."

Three weeks later, I left the hospital on crutches. Before I left, I asked him why, if my goring was like that of Manolete, had I survived.

"That was ten years ago," he said. "We didn't have all the information then that we have now, that we learned from the war."

I thanked him. He shrugged and said, "You'll have an interesting scar now to show at cocktail parties."

Then a phone call came and he hurried off: Ordóñez had been gored in Sevilla, and he had to catch a plane immediately.

And so I returned to San Francisco and the quiet life of El Matador. Occasionally, when well-taken with wine and encouraged by curious El Matador customers, I would drop my pants to display the wound, just as the doctor had suggested.

On Sunday evenings at El Matador we showed bullfighting movies. It was a popular institution: Juan Buckingham would play his flamenco guitar, and when there was no soundtrack, I would narrate the films. We showed the immortals of the bullring, from Belmonte and Joselito to Manolete and Ortega. And, of course, the Mexican genius, Carlos Arruza .

I met Carlos in 1944, when he first arrived in Spain virtually unknown, and watched his meteoric ascent to the top of the bullfighting world in a matter of weeks. Twelve years later I had the privilege of helping him write his fine book, *My Life as a Matador.*

Probably the most popular and versatile torero Mexico has produced, he was Manolete's greatest rival from 1944 to 1946. Completely the opposite of the staid, serious Spaniard Manolete, Arruza was carefree, good-looking, and wild, with a rare sense of humor. Once the movie director and bullfighting expert Budd Boetticher asked matador Luis Miguel Domínguín to name the ten best living bullfighters. Domínguín said, "I must put myself first, of course. Then comes Pepe Luis Vázquez, then Domingo Ortega, then . . . " and he reeled off his list. When he finished, Boetticher said, "But you didn't mention Arruza." Domínguín sneered and dismissed his hated rival with, "That *acrobat!*" Boetticher then went to Arruza and put the same question to him.

"Well," said the matador, "I wouldn't stay in this business if I didn't think I was the best. But there are many fine toreros," and he named them.

Boetticher said, "You didn't mention Domínguín."

"Hey Budd!" said Arruza. "You said ten, not feefty!"

One day in 1956, Arruza telephoned from Mexico City to say he wanted to visit San Francisco for the first time, causing great excitement at El Matador. During the conversation he said he was "scared of the *terremotos,* the earthquakes," and asked how often we had them.

It was interesting to hear one of the bravest bullfighters of all times use the word "scared"—he who had been gored thirteen times; he who had invented the dangerous *arrucina* pass, where the muleta cape is held *behind* the legs instead of in front, and the suicidal *péndulo* pass, where the lure is not only held behind the body but swung back and forth before the charge; he who used to casually rest his elbow between the bull's horns in the "*teléfono*" *adorno;* he who in the 1945 season took part in 108 amazing corridas, killed 222 bulls, and was awarded a record 217 ears, 73 tails, and 20 hooves.

In vain did I assure him that we hadn't had an earthquake in years and that getting one during his visit was a one-in-a-million chance. He wasn't convinced, such was his phobia, and he checked into a motel on flat Lombard Street instead of a hotel on Nob Hill, "which will certainly fall down when the *terremoto* strikes."

He came with several friends, and that first night they whooped it up quite a bit at El Matador. We showed movies of some of his great fights in Spain, and Carlos watched intently. When he saw himself prepare for a very dangerous pass with a bull in Sevilla, he warned the screen, "Hey, Charlie, look out. Don' do that. Look out, you gonna get tossed!" When the animal did indeed catch and toss him, he slumped back in his seat, saying, "I tol' you so, you crazy fool!" Finally, they all called it a night and returned to their motel in, well, high spirits. After getting into bed, Arruza spotted a coin machine next to it. Thinking it was for music, he dropped in a quarter, turned out the light, and lay back. It was one of those massage machines, and instead of hearing soothing melodies, Arruza felt the earth shake, rock, and quiver.

"*Terremoto!*" he yelled, leaping out of bed. Arruza ran out the door to warn his companions and continued till he was out in the street, where he shamefacedly discovered there was no earthquake.

Mark Twain said that we are all ignorant but on different subjects; he could have added that we're all cowards but about different things.

I last saw Carlos in May 1966, two weeks before he died. We had dinner with him in Mexico City. Astonishingly, at forty-six he was on top of the world. He was in great physical shape and had just put on one of the finest exhibitions of his life in the biggest ring in the world, in Mexico City; he had a pretty wife and three children and a lovely ranch outside the city. When he kissed my wife good-bye, he said he'd see us soon since he was going to perform in Tijuana.

I telephoned in two weeks to make sure he was fighting. "Carlos should be here any minute," said Mari, his wife. "He's been out at the ranch."

An hour later, when a phone call came from Mexico City, I said, "Carlos?"

"No," said a choked male voice. "I'm not Carlos."

"Well, can you tell me if he's fighting Sunday?"

"No, he's not, not fighting."

"When will he be fighting?"

"*Nunca!*" The voice cracked with sobs. "Never!"

Mexico's idol, the man who had been gored so many times, who had survived encounters with some two thousand bulls, had been killed on a rainy day when a bus crashed head on into his car on the Toluca highway.

Part Four

No matter what one does for a living, but especially running a nightclub and often drinking more than one should, ultimately one's health and psyche wear down. In 1959 I was ready for a long break: Could it be that there was life outside of the Barbary Coast, North Beach, and El Matador?

One night Nancy Rutgers, the daughter of James Norman Hall, co-author of *Mutiny on the Bounty*, came into the Matador with her husband and a charming part-Tahitian woman named Purea Reasin. Their tales of Tahiti were so beguiling that I there and then decided to desert my saloon for a few months and try the languid way of life on their island, that island that many people think is "near Hawaii"; in actuality, Tahiti is as far from Hawaii as Hawaii is from California.

Until 1960, when an air strip was constructed by filling in the lagoon at Faaa, Tahiti was blessedly very remote from the outside world. For example, when I first went there in 1959, the trip took nine days from California by steamship. Upon arrival in Papeete, I was given a welcoming party by the Rutgers, a splendid luau in their hilltop home in the Arue district. Among the guests was a tall, bald man with a long beard and a Scandinavian accent.

"Vell, and how are you liking our Tahiti?"

"Fine," I said, "but I didn't realize that it would take nine whole days without even seeing land to get here."

"Vell," he said, "it took me three months without seeing land to get here."

"Lord, how'd you come," I asked, "by freighter?"

"No," he replied with a twinkle. "By Kon Tiki."

Indeed he did—he was Bengt Danielsson, the distinguished anthropologist and author who came by the raft Kon Tiki to Polynesia, fell in love with Tahiti, and never left. I was to become his neighbor in the Paea district for that wonderful summer and during the following one, and on five subsequent trips.

Many people who have visited Tahiti in recent years have told me they are disappointed with the island's modernization. All I can say to them is, "You should have been there in the old days, when there were virtually no cars, no stoplights, no big hotels, when the Tahitians weren't jaded by tourism, and only a handful of Americans—all characters—lived there."

The characters—ah, the characters in Tahiti in those days. It was something like this: Every day you sit on the quai at the sidewalk café Vaima and sip your rum and discuss who slept with whom the night before, watching the never-ending parade of people:

Ripley Gooding, in his big hat, strides jauntily by, smiling his good, horsey smile and looking exactly like the model for *South Pacific*'s planter Émile de Becque. Part Tahitian, part Bostonian, he was one of the most active men on the island, and his Lotus Village was one of the better bungalow-type hotels outside Papeete. He used to own a popular night spot in San Francisco at 99 Broadway, just down from El Matador, called the Tahitian Hut; I painted the murals in it when I was seventeen.

The French baron, who gave up a château in Burgundy for a grass hut, strolls by hand in hand with his saronged *vahine.* Nancy Rutgers comes from market staggering under the weight of a tuna fish, and a few feet away Henry Taft, a grandson of the twenty-sixth president of the United States, ties up his small sailboat, in which he'd come from Honolulu. Smollin, a distinguished-looking general, late of the Czar's Army, shops in a Chinese store. In front of the Bar Lea, maestro André Kostelanetz has a local musician cornered, trying to find out why there's no minor key music on the island. He is temporarily distracted when a gorgeous Tahitian woman strolls by in a Dior dress. And there with her—wonder of wonders— is Herb Caen, a long way from his San Francisco beat.

Then there's the eccentric Hungarian painter who paints only one thing: the island Mooréa. He's been here for twelve years, and all he paints is that island a few miles away. He paints it at dawn, at sunset, when it's clear, when it rains. "Why should I paint anything else?" he growls. "It is my conscience."

Eddie Lund, an American who years ago came to Tahiti and did more for recording and assembling native music than anyone else, stops his little car and gets out, his monkey, Nanette, on his shoulder, his pet piglet, Joe Sheppard, on a fancy leash. "Joe's had a cold," he says as he puts Vicks up its nose.

And finally, the American millionaire down the beach from my house hates noise, and every dawn his native neighbors' roosters wake him up. So he has his butler buy them all and kill them. Soon a new crop and another and another appear, and he has these killed also. He never knew that he was the greatest single outlet for the rooster market in all Polynesia.

Though often cheerful, Tahitians weren't the "happy natives" depicted in Hollywood films, and their lives were ruled by superstition. For instance, our cook, Jacques, buried his father; a few days later, the villagers were horrified to find that his coffin had pushed up through the shallow earth and remained at a forty-five-degree angle. Suddenly, many people fell ill, and there were no fish to be caught. For weeks there were no fish.

"It is the work of *tupapa'u*," said the witch doctor, "the ghosts." He told Jacques that his father had cast an evil spell before dying, and there was only one way he could break it: "You must go at night to the cemetery and stab your father."

So at midnight Jacques went to the graveyard, opened his father's coffin, and stabbed him several times. Then they buried the coffin again, people got well, and the fish came back.

"Wasn't it a hard thing to do?" I asked.

He shrugged. "I had to do what the medicine man said. Besides, I hated my father."

Marlon Brando lived near my house in the outskirts of Papeete while MGM was in Tahiti filming the remake of *Mutiny on the Bounty,* and the colony was so small then that we would see each other often. One day he would be charming and friendly, the next time aloof and brooding. Tarita Teriipia, the pretty fry cook from the Hotel Tahiti, was spotted by the producers and given the main female role in the film. Marlon ended up marrying her. Tarita was always prompt on the set and diligent, but the other Tahitian actors, and the hundreds of extras, were not. At their whim, they would become *fiu,* the Tahitian word for "bored" and "fed up," and after a few days of shooting they would take off, leaving the director, Lewis Milestone, frustrated, forcing him to redesign shots and set-ups and costing the company millions. Then Brando and Tarita came up with a splendid solution: they had MGM send two dentists down from Los Angeles. The Tahitians, because of their diet or lack of minerals, were nearly always lacking teeth, and they coveted false teeth more than anything. Accordingly, MGM had all the extras fitted with dentures, which they were required to turn in after each day's shooting; at the end of filming the picture—if they hadn't missed a day's work—they would own the teeth.

It worked like a charm.

Marlon—"Mahr-law" to the Tahitians—subsequently bought the little island of Tetiaroa and still spends time on it, away from the limelight.

A fter three idyllic months in Tahiti, I came back to the smoky nights of North Beach. On one of those nights Gauguin came in—not *the* Gauguin, but his son Émile, whom I had met in Papeete.

One of the most depressing documents I've ever seen is in the Paul Gauguin museum in Tahiti. When Gauguin, impoverished at the age of fifty-five, died in 1903 on the island of Nuku Hiva, the Tahitian police confiscated his paintings for an outstanding fifty dollar fine for drunken rowdiness. The document lists now-famous paintings and carvings being sold for a few francs. Many did not sell and were destroyed, such as, "One large picture of three *vahines* in *pareus* on the beach: no bids, burned," and so forth.

As with his friend Van Gogh, it took a long time for Gauguin's genius to be recognized. When he returned to Paris after his first stay in Tahiti, he expected to have a triumphant and lucrative exhibition. Instead, the great paintings that we esteem so highly today were ridiculed, and only one sold—to his fellow painter and friend Degas.

Only after his death did Gauguin's work become appreciated—and lucrative. Somerset Maugham tells of going to Tahiti in the 1920s looking for works by Gauguin. At a grass hut in the Punauia district where Gauguin once lived, he discovered a superb pair of doors carved by Gauguin. He offered the Tahitian who lived there the equivalent of a few dollars for the doors. The man refused, and Maugham upped the price.

"No, no," shrugged the man, to whom Gauguin meant nothing. "I would just have to buy new doors and have them installed."

Maugham came back the next day with two new doors and a carpenter, and the man agreed to give him the doors for less than a hundred dollars. Today, those doors are worth a million dollars and can be seen in one of London's most prestigious museums.

When I went to Tahiti, people would ask me semi-seriously to "try to find a little Gauguin for me."

I soon discovered that there were no Gauguin paintings or drawings or carvings to be found on the island, even in the little museum. Only Gauguin's son had remained.

Émile Gauguin was the son of Paul Gauguin and his Tahitian "wife" (he had left a legitimate Danish wife and children in Europe). Tall and hawk-nosed, Émile was a Polynesian and very fat version of his father. He was the only beggar on the island, and when people were at church in Papeete, he would steal the loaves of bread from the baskets on their bicycles. He was often jailed for that and for being *taero*—drunk and obnoxious. His only enterprise was to occasionally make bamboo fish traps. I would see him almost every day and would give him a few francs. He was friendly, rather infantile, and when he passed by in his shorts and his huge bare belly, Tahitians would tap their heads. "*Il y a des chambres à louer,*" they'd say. "There are rooms for rent there."

In 1960, when the airstrip was put in, tourists came to Tahiti in droves. Émile soon learned that being the only genuine Gauguin on the island was a commodity, and he would sell his autograph, painstakingly scratched out, for five francs. For ten francs, he would make a childish drawing of a palm tree, and tourists could take it home as a joke: "Look, Mabel, I brought you a real Gauguin from Tahiti."

An enterprising woman from Chicago somehow talked Émile into going back home with her. The long plane trip both terrified and fascinated him, as did the big city. She installed him in an apartment, bought canvases and paint, and taught him how to draw a crude outrigger on a beach fringed with palm trees. Then she taught him to color the drawings with thin washes of oil color and put his signature in the corner—voilà! Instant Gauguins.

Apparently, the canvases sold well at a nice price. Émile enjoyed the money, split fifty-fifty, and the novelty of living in America. There was nothing illegal about it: the paintings were sold as genuine Gauguins, but as E. Gauguins, not P. Gauguins. *Caveat emptor.* But he soon got *fiu,* fed up, and terribly homesick. So he took his earnings and bought a ticket back to Tahiti, stopping in San Francisco on the way. That's when he waddled in to see me in the Matador.

"You miss the sunsets, I'm sure," I suggested, "and the free way of life, and the loving *vahines,* and the view of Mooréa beyond the lagoon. God, I miss them myself."

"No, I miss the *poe,*" he said, referring to the Tahitian taro dessert. "And the breadfruit and the *poisson cru* and the roast pig and the Hinano beer, that's what I miss."

He left the next day for his island paradise and never painted again.

Sterling Hayden liked bars and came into El Matador often. But it was a little too fancy for his taste; he liked his saloons a little more saloony. He preferred places where the clients had fish scales on their clothes and argued about sloops, westerlies, and scrimshaw. Secondly an actor, he was first and always a deep-water captain, a seeker, a wanderer.

Tahiti had stayed on my mind, and the following year I again deserted the Matador and its smoky nights for another three-month stay on that then-blessed isle. But in a way, the bloom was off the *tiare*—Tahiti seemed less wonderful than during my first visit. I became like all the other people who said "You shoulda been here in the old days"—Maugham, Rupert Brooke, Robert Louis Stevenson. Even Captain Cook, the first Englishman to sail to Tahiti, complained on his second trip that Tahiti was ruined compared to his first time! The new airport under construction was partly the cause of my feelings, for it seemed symptomatic, presaging the doom of the carefree Tahiti of yore. Still, I loved the place and met several interesting people while completing a book there called, daringly, *Tahiti.*

This time, the most compelling and charismatic character I came to know was Sterling Hayden.

Most people know Sterling Hayden as a renegade actor, a former matinee idol, who played "character" roles in such good films as *Doctor Strangelove, The Killing,* and *The Godfather* and leading roles in such bad films as *Virginia* and *The Iron Sheriff.* But those who read his two books, *Wanderer* and *Voyage,* know that he was also a writer of the sea to be compared with Melville and Joseph Conrad. And to those who knew him personally, he was a larger-than-life, troubled, unique, searching, and compelling man.

In 1960, he defied a court order, "kidnapped" his four children, and, as an outlaw, sailed off with them to Tahiti in his ancient ninety-six-foot schooner, "Wanderer." Before becoming a Hollywood actor, Sterling had been a Grand Banks fisherman and had done a lot of sailing around Gloucester, Massachusetts, and around the world. At twenty-two, he had become the youngest man to earn captain's papers and was considered one of the great deep-water sailors of the world. When his huge schooner, all sails up, flew into Papeete harbor, hundreds of people came to watch. Generally, a boat of this size comes in under power and escorted by a pilot boat. Never had anyone seen such a large schooner enter with all sails up, drop anchor, drop all sails but the mainsail, and with no power but the wind, *back* into the slip. A great roar went up from the crowd as they watched. Sterling later confessed to me with a boyish grin, "I might have looked cool and calm when we warped her into the quay, but I had my finger on the motor's ignition the whole time, ready to kick 'er in!"

Sterling rented a thatched bungalow near our house in the Paea district, and we saw him virtually every day for three months. We sailed with him over to Mooréa, and it was a pleasure to watch him in his element, booming commands to his first mate, the hairless, Queequeg-like Spike Africa, or helping his crew hoist the sails or winch up the anchor (no motorized gizmos allowed on *this* ship!). Although forty-three years old and 6'5", he climbed the rigging quicker and better than any of the young crew.

We introduced him to a nubile Tahitian-Peruvian girl with the improbable name of Nita Wanamaker, and they hit it off. Sterling seemed content, and the tight lines around the corners of his mouth softened. He would stay in this Tahitian paradise forever, he said. One evening, he brought a large, unfinished manuscript to me and shyly, almost apologetically, asked if I'd read it. I sat up all night with it. I was astounded. The antithesis of the self-serving Hollywood memoir, it was a reflective autobiography built into the framework of the kidnapping and the long hazardous sail from San Francisco to Tahiti—revealing, exciting, and splendidly written. I encouraged him in every way and urged him to finish it.

Though he told me he was happier than he'd ever been in his life, he seemed to have, as someone once said about Robert Louis Stevenson, "an incapacity for happiness." Was it because his father died when Sterling was nine? Or because his first love was a lost love—the nineteen-year-old daughter of the American Consul in Tahiti when he was twenty-three and sailing around the world on a clipper ship? Or because he'd abandoned the sea and "sold out" to Hollywood? Or was he simply one of those people doomed to congenital unhappiness?

Kitty Hayden, Sterling's last wife, is convinced that the actor was bedeviled by guilt and self-loathing because he cooperated with the government when testifying before the Un-American Activities Committee in the fifties. "He never forgave himself for doing this, and it haunted him from 1951 until the end of his life," she wrote me in May of 1991. "The main reason he testified is that he knew he was going to try to get custody of his children and knew it would be impossible if he didn't cooperate. Three weeks after you saw Sterling for the last time [in 1986, shortly before his death] he gave a long taped interview for the BBC in which he discussed in depth his shame and guilt over this appearance."

One night in Tahiti he seemed unusually restless and self-critical, and I remember his quoting F. Scott Fitzgerald: "In the dark hour of the soul it is always three in the morning, and you are the only one awake . . . "

After a few months Sterling began finding fault with Tahiti, Nita, and his life there. One day I bumped into Nita in downtown Papeete, and when I asked how Sterling was, she frowned and said evasively, "*Il est très dur. Il faut que j'aille*—I must leave." A new woman, Betsy Pickering, an American model, had entered his life. She had been visiting Tahiti when she "jumped ship" to stay with him for several months. Always restless, he went back to America with his children and finished the book, *Wanderer,* which was published to great acclaim. This gave him enormous satisfaction, as he'd never thought of himself as an actor and was always faintly embarrassed to be called one. He gave me one of the first copies, and I treasure the inscription: "To B.C. who said—long before anyone else—join The Club, you bastard, you can write—in memory of an island night and many a mainland night. . . . "

Years after the publication of *Wanderer,* he wrote:

I found it rather strange, once the book was published, that folks on occasion would say, "But why did you write this book?" With some even asking, "Was it to find yourself?" As though, before the writing, I had been lost, which of course I was—and remained so

after the book was accomplished, and am now, fourteen years later, and confidently expect to be for the
remainder of my time.

Lost, indeed! Don't talk to me about finding yourself. Only as you are lost is there any hope for you.
Which is what, again, wandering is all about. . . . Hell,
I never felt lost at sea, even when I didn't know precisely where on earth the vessel was. I was making a
hundred and fifty dollars a month as master of a sailing
ship when I tossed it over and landed in Hollywood
making two-fifty per week with a contract that led to
five or six thousand a week at some distant date. Then
it was I learned what lostness was.

For the rest of his life he continued to flirt with Hollywood, especially when he needed some quick money, but
it was writing that occupied his time. In the early sixties,
he married Kitty Devine, who became a lovely and adoring
wife, and though they had a fine home in Connecticut, he
hated the idea of suburbia and spent a lot of his time alone
aboard his remodeled barge in Paris, or going through the
canals of France or Holland—seeking, always seeking.

Once I quoted to him from a letter written by Dickens
toward the end of the author's life: "Why is it a sense always comes crushing upon me now, as of one happiness I
have missed in life and one friend and companion I have
never made?"

Sterling said immediately, "That's me, that's me!"

He came into the Matador often, and we'd kill a bottle
over several hours of solving the world's problems and
reminiscing about Tahiti, which, of course, had already
become "the good old days."

He had an incredible capacity for what W. C. Fields
called "espiritus fermentae," and in later years he grew
worried when his intake increased. Knowing I'd given the
stuff up, he once telephoned me from France asking for
advice on how to cut down. "Start by limiting yourself," I
said. "Limit yourself to one bottle a day." Sterling was

quiet for a moment. Then he offered a classic, but serious, riposte, "But what would I do in the afternoon?" Eventually, he managed to cut way back on alcohol and somewhat on "grass," but never completely. His last years were spent in a house on a hill overlooking Sausalito harbor, with regular visits to Kitty and the children in Connecticut. He was a charismatic and anachronistic figure as he strode around the hills in his black cut-off jeans, his long, gray biblical beard, carrying a walking staff and a pouch of "Lebanese Red" hashish hung defiantly around his neck. The image was a far cry, purposefully it seemed, from the golden boy who had made romantic films with the beauteous Madeleine Carroll so long ago, when Paramount's publicity had billed him as "The Most Beautiful Man in the Movies."

In 1986, he became very ill. As Herb Caen later wrote in a splendid obituary:

> We knew for months that Sterling was dying but, to borrow the excruciating last words of another great friend, Bill Saroyan, we thought an exception would be made in his case. Sterling had cancer, but he was bigger than life and would beat it, somehow, some way.

And it certainly looked as though he might. We shared the same birthday, and on that day I flew up from Santa Barbara to see him at his house. He was brave as hell and though gaunt and moving painfully and slowly, his voice was strong and optimistic. He reminisced cheerfully about Tahiti and Gloucester—and the war. He rarely spoke of his wartime experiences, though he was a bonafide Marine hero, having parachuted some eleven times, fighting with the Yugoslav partisans in the mountains, and carrying arms under sail at night from Italy to Yugoslavia. But this day he told a funny story about the war and Madeleine Carroll, the actress who was often called the most beautiful woman in the world:

"I was sent back to Paris for some R and R and saw in the paper that Madeleine Carroll was in town. We were heading for divorce and hadn't seen each other for a couple of years but I thought it would be fun to take her out. I called her one evening at her hotel apartment and a man answered. 'I'd like to speak to Miss Carroll, please.' The man said, 'May I ask your name?' I answered, 'What's yours?' The man answered, 'General Dwight Eisenhower.'" Sterling chuckled. "I hung up."

During the last days a serenity came over him. He was confined to bed in a dreamy, calm state. But late one night he suddenly sat up in bed and boomed, "Jesus, I'm dying—I gotta get out of here! The ship's on fire!"

He pulled away the various tubes attached to him, and before his wife could stop him, he leapt out of bed and, in his flannel nightgown, lurched out to the front porch. Before he could get to the road, Kitty grabbed him by the night shirt, hung on, and with the help of two neighbors, they managed to get him back to his room where he collapsed.

The last paragraph of Herb Caen's obituary for Sterling on May 26, 1986, was this:

"Got no whales but had one hell of a fine sail," he once
said about his life, quoting a Nantucket shipmaster. The
fine sail ended Friday morning in his little wooden
house up the hill from Sally Stanford's old Valhalla.
Valhalla, yes, and funeral pyres for a bearded wanderer.
When he found out he had the big sickness and
wouldn't get out alive, he said, "Well, it's the next
adventure, right?" He said it in the booming voice that
reverberates in my ears right now. Have a fine sail,
Sterbo.

His longtime friend Lewis Vogler summed up Sterling's death mournfully and succinctly, "Huge presence, huge absence."

Sterling Hayden, the actor, may end up as only a foot-note in future film encyclopedias, but I firmly believe that Hayden's book *Wanderer* will last as long as people care about adventures at sea and soul-searching autobiogra-phy. Here is the last page of that fine book. "He" is himself, of course, and he is in Sausalito saying a final good-bye to his beloved schooner, which he must sell.

Then, slitting the cap on a bottle of aquavit, he poured a proper blend and sat on a fo'c'sle bench. He heard the moan in the rigging as he looked at the beams and the kness and the massive bole of the foremast. He drained his mug and poured. His narrowed eyes now filled with a pageant of fo'c'sle faces, faces of sailormen swept from the seas by Time. He looked in the coffin-sized bunks quarried deep in the hull and heard the laughter of children.

He stands by the wheel for most of a helmsman's hour, entranced at times by the dim-lit compass rose. Then he palms the emptied bottle and hurls it into the bay. Grabbing his bag, he slips over the bulwarks and down to the heaving logs where, under the tall ship's lee, he turns and stares at the legend:

WANDERER
SAN FRANCISCO

With his back to the wind he plows up the dock and reaching the land turns left. He corners the squat brown bank, crosses the Bridgeway Road, turns right past The Tides bookstore, and steps from the storm to the warmth of the No Name Bar.

He buys a drink and turns to a ship lost in the night and drinks to a life that was.

He turns to stare at a face in the back-bar mirror: a vague face with bleak and querulous eyes. The eyes lock and he drinks to himself alone. Vale! Wanderer.

While the full-length portrait of Manolete dominated the entranceway, another bullfighter's presence also permeated El Matador. He was Juan Belmonte, whose suit of lights was displayed behind the bar to the left of the bull's head. Gold and crimson and tarnished— how small it looked, how long the sleeves. One would have thought it belonged to a young boy, not the greatest bullfighter of all Spain. Next to it was the charcoal portrait I'd done of his craggy face in 1945 in Sevilla. Frequently people ask, "Who was the greatest matador—Belmonte, Joselito, or Manolete?" That is like asking, "Who was the greatest flyer—Orville Wright, Lindbergh, or Doolittle?" Belmonte invented what all other fighters after him have had to imitate in some way.

One of the greatest breaks of my life was meeting Juan Belmonte. I was twenty-one, a vice-consul in the Sevilla Consulate, and I had bull fever. I had fought in Mexico a few times when I was an art student. In the lobby of the elegant old Alfonso XIII Hotel, someone pointed out the Great Man to me, I asked to be introduced, and Belmonte was immediately amused by the presumption of a would-be yanqui torero. He invited me to his ranch for the *tientas,* and then under his long tutelage I began to realize how little I knew. Three years later I appeared on the same program with him, the supreme thrill of my life. He meant a lot to me. I'd even considered naming my eldest son Juan Belmonte Conrad.

It had been so many years since I'd seen him. As I sat in my saloon staring at his likeness, I kept thinking that time was running out though he was not yet seventy. I kept telling myself drop everything, go see him.

Then in the spring of 1962, I had the closest thing to a presentiment I've ever experienced. "Pack up," I said to my wife. "We're going to Spain—I want to see Belmonte before it's too late." We did not arrive in time. We were in

the air when it happened; we saw the shocking headlines
in the newspapers in the Madrid airport when we landed.

All aficionados know the story of his life through his
autobiography and Hemingway's *Death in the Afternoon*—
he was purely and simply the greatest bullfighter of this
century. But I wonder how many know about his death. It
took me many hours and many interviews to reconstruct
that last incredible day.

It was Sunday morning, April 8, 1962, and he went to church as on any other Sunday. Whether or not he knew it then, this was to be the last morning of his life. He was a very small man with a great barracuda jaw and deep-set, piercing eyes. He had all the rewards that any man could aspire to in this life, yet he would cause his own death before this day was over.

He came out of the chapel of San José, blinking in the already hot Sevilla sun, holding his hat to his chest. Several of the crowd leaving Mass said, *"Buenos dias, Don Juan,"* and it was almost reverential the way they said it. He did not know most of them, but they knew him. Indeed all of Spain and Portugal and Mexico and South America knew him. He was much more than just a famous and rich bullfighter: he was the most idolized and legendary figure that Spain had produced since El Cid.

Now just six days away from his seventieth birthday, he did not look anywhere near that age. Not that he was young looking—he had never looked young. But his hair was graying only slightly, his jaw was still thrust out defiantly, and his scarred face didn't look much different than it had ever looked. Only his eyes—eyes that no one ever forgot once he'd seen them—showed the secret hurts of his soul.

He put on his hat, a mushroom sort of hat, and started toward his car in that special walk of his that was not quite a shuffle. (Once, four decades earlier, when he was at the peak of his career, he had said, "My legs are in such a terrible state that if one wants to move it has to request permission from the other." That was long ago, and the legs were no better now.)

His chauffeur, Antonio, held the front door of the black Vedette open, and Belmonte stepped in. With all his millions of pesetas, he was quite content to be driven in this modest car. In the back seat was Asunción, his old housekeeper of many years. The chauffeur got behind the steering wheel, and they drove off.

"Across the r-r-river," Belmonte said.

"*Si, Don Juan,*" said the chauffeur. No further address was necessary.

They drove past the Cristina Hotel, in the back of which Belmonte had his large apartment, then across the bridge over the muddy Guadalquivir. This was the same river that Belmonte had swum across at night as a ragged urchin more than half a century before to fight the bulls in the open fields, the fields where he first developed the style that would rock the bullfighting world, where he had first pitted his puny body against the great bulls. It was also the same river where he had slaved as a dredger, his belly empty and his head full of dreams of someday being a matador. To the right was the squalid district of Triana, where Belmonte was brought up, the eldest of thirteen children, where he had seen his brothers and sisters taken off to the poorhouse because there wasn't enough to eat.

But that was way in the past. Now Belmonte's car drove to the new district of Los Remedios and stopped in front of a handsome apartment building. Belmonte got out of the car, taking with him a package from the glove compartment. It contained 400,000 pesetas, which he had withdrawn from the bank the day before. He went up in the elevator to the third floor. He knocked, and Enriqueta Pérez Lora opened the door. He had given the apartment to her, and it was filled with photos of him. She was about thirty-five years old, brown haired, handsome, and sad-eyed. She had been a governess for one of his daughters when he had fallen in love with her a dozen years before. She had been so beautiful. Her face was still smooth and unlined, but she was getting plump.

No one knows what was said or done in the hour he spent with her; Enriqueta refuses to discuss any phase of their long relationship.

Afterward, he and the chauffeur drove along the river out toward Utrera. It was hotter now, and the flat wheat fields shimmered on either side of the road. They could see the hills where, years ago, some rabid aficionados had carved a giant likeness of Belmonte's profile in the cliffs, and one could still make it out. In forty-five minutes they came to the big olive groves that stretched as far as the eye could see. This was the beginning of Belmonte's property, the four-thousand-acre ranch Gómez Cardeña, the vast tangible reward of more than a thousand afternoons in the ring. When the car reached the white stone gates, it turned left down the dirt road that led to the big, white, stucco house. They passed the foreman of the ranch; Belmonte called out of the window to him: "Let's go! Be ready in ten minutes."

She said with alarm, "But Don Juan, you are not supposed to!"

He didn't answer.

The chauffeur parked the car in the cobbled courtyard, and Belmonte went into the house the back way and into the big master bedroom. He changed from his suit into the grey trousers and bolero jacket of his *traje carto,* the Spanish rancher's costume. He pulled on his boots and strapped on his *zajones,* the ornate leather chaps. He took his flat-brimmed *sombrero cordobés* off the peg in the hall and went out into the courtyard, where his superbly trained and favorite horse, Maravilla, was saddled and waiting, held by one of the stable boys. Belmonte stroked the animal's neck and chest for a long time, talking to it lovingly and letting it nuzzle him. Then the stable boy gave him a leg up into the saddle. The foreman, Diego Mateos, was there also on his horse, and they smiled warmly at each other. He'd been with Belmonte for twenty years. Wordlessly, the two men trotted out of the courtyard, each holding one of the long wooden lances of *derribando,* the ancient sport of painlessly toppling cattle. Belmonte didn't look like much on a horse—any more than he did on foot—but over the years he had made himself into one of the greatest horsemen in the world. He loved riding after the cattle better than anything else, and when the doctors had recently vetoed that activity, it had shriveled and demeaned him in his own eyes.

In twenty minutes, they found the heifers they were looking for in one of the open fields. The heifers were three years old, big, with sharp horns curving forward and up. Belmonte pointed at one of them with his lance and kicked his horse, and the foreman dashed ahead to cut the heifer away from the others. The two horsemen pursued it down a small gulley and up across the flats.

Belmonte was in the lead, holding the lance in tilting position. It had to be done just right. He came up behind the heifer fast. Then, judging the timing exactly, he jabbed the blunt end of the pole to the left of the animal's tail bone, just as the hind legs were on the rise. It was done perfectly; the heifer, knocked off its stride, pitched forward and did a somersault.

It scrambled to its feet, snorting with anger. Instead of fleeing, it charged the first thing that it saw, which was the foreman's horse. The man deftly spurred his trained animal in a tight circle and avoided the charge of the furious heifer. Then it attacked Belmonte's horse, and Belmonte zigzagged away, trailing the lance in the dirt behind him as a target for the heifer to hook at. Finally, the heifer stopped and whirled around, defying anyone to come close enough for her to reach him with her horns. The men pulled up their horses thirty feet away.

"*Muy brava*," said the foreman. "A brave one."

"Lovely and brave," said Belmonte. "Give me the muleta."

The foreman hesitated. "But Don Juan, the doctor . . . "

"Give me the muleta." Belmonte repeated the command in a soft voice, one that could not be disobeyed. He got off his horse and held out his hand. There were tears in Mateos's eyes as he reluctantly untied the thongs that held a fake sword and the red cloth, the muleta, to the back of the saddle. Belmonte took the flannel in his left hand and then flared it out and spread it wide over the wooden sword in his right hand. He shook it twice to get the feel of it, and then he walked toward the heifer.

He walked casually, not gracefully, round-shouldered, an old man out for a stroll on old legs. With his left hand he held onto the upper part of his jacket, as an after-dinner speaker might, and his right hand absently trailed the muleta in the dust. The animal studied the approaching man. Then it lowered its head and charged hard at his legs. When it was seven feet away, Belmonte calmly dragged the muleta up from behind his body, parallel to his legs, offering the cloth as a target. The animal swerved off to the left after this new lure.

Then, a strange transformation occurred. Belmonte's body, which had been relaxed and slumped, suddenly stiffened and straightened gracefully, and he seemed to grow as the animal charged. His back arched; he went up on the point of his left foot in the classic, beautiful, old-fashioned way. He swung the muleta lure inches in front of the heifer's horns, and his arm seemed to extend beyond what was physically possible, so that the animal was led past the man's body as though its nose were sewn to the cloth.

"*Olé!*" shouted the foreman, forgetting the passage of years, forgetting the matador's age, lost in familiar admiration for the man's skill.

When the heifer realized it had hit nothing solid, it wheeled and charged. Belmonte was waiting for it, the muleta spread wide like a sail in front of him. As the animal charged from the right, Belmonte drew the cloth across his body, his whole torso going through with the charge, *cargando la suerte,* the horn grazing his waist. No longer was he an infirm old man—now he was a graceful, regal, magical hypnotist.

"*Olé!*" cried the foreman, as though he'd never before seen the master in action, as though he were in the audience at a bullring.

Fifteen more passes Belmonte gave the animal, controlling it perfectly, the wooden sword spreading the folds of the cloth. Then he took the sword out, tempting the baffled heifer with only half the earlier target. Finally, he lurched away from the animal, leaving it completely dominated, its gray tongue out. Sweaty and panting, but flushed with pleasure, Belmonte came over to his horse and put his forehead down on the sheepskin-covered saddle.

Now Mateos could no longer forget. The mirage he'd seen vanished, an illusion of the youth and grandeur that had been and was no longer.

"Enough, Don Juan," Mateos whispered prayerfully under his breath. "Enough."

"No," Belmonte coughed, "no, not enough."

He got on his horse and cantered off to cut another heifer from the herd.

Six more animals Belmonte fought like this. But the encounters took their toll. Pale, trembling, and wet with sweat, he once again became an old man, hauling himself into the saddle after the final heifer.

Belmonte took a longer way home, riding slowly through fields he had not seen in months, as though wanting to check every last foot of his beloved ranch—the ranch on which he had fought bulls, illegally and at night by the light of a stolen lantern, when he was a ragged, hungry boy.

When he got back to the courtyard, the foreman was already there. "Don Juan, is there anything else I can do for you?"

Belmonte shook his head, and suddenly his eyes were moist. "No, Mateos, no. Nothing. Thank you for everything."

Belmonte turned and went into the house. Wearily, he took off his chaps and his jacket and shirt. He put on the yellow top of a pair of pajamas and his faded brown bathrobe, in the right-hand pocket of which there was a hard object, a small pistol he kept against intruders.

He went from his bedroom into the big living room, white and handsomely decorated in the simple style of an aristocratic Andaluz ranch. There were no bulls' heads, no faded posters, no crossed swords as in most retired matadors' houses. There were books—a great many books, books on every subject, and all of them read and reread by this extraordinary man who had had only two years of schooling. At least a dozen of the books were about Belmonte himself. One of them, *Killer of Bulls* by Chavez Nogales, says in the introduction by Leslie Charleris: "If, without ever having heard of Belmonte, you were told that a man who was practically a cripple, who was certainly a physical wreck, could become the greatest bullfighter in the world, would you not say that if he did, it would be performing a miracle?"

Around the room were photos of his grandchildren, his son, his daughters—and a photo of Julia, his estranged wife, looking cool and aristocratic and reproachful in her house in Madrid. And on a bookcase was a photo of Belmonte with the King of Spain in 1917. The King, with his hand on Belmonte's shoulder, is looking flushed and proud, since he'd just seen Belmonte put up one of the greatest fights in Madrid's history.

There was the photo of Joselito, the week before he was killed in the arena at Talavera. And there was a photo of Joselito's brother, Rafael, "El Gallo"—the bald, pathetic, appealing, indispensable friend of Belmonte's youth who'd died only two years ago. And Lord, how the old man, Rafael, had lingered and suffered and whimpered and dribbled his food on himself as he lay there in bed and tried to feed himself. Joselito had been luckier, much luckier.

There was the photo of Belmonte's sixteen-year-old grandson, his best friend, the one who was determined to be a matador, the only one who would ride with him whenever he wanted and who liked to tilt the cattle with him and hear how it was in the old days. But they'd taken him far away to school, and now there was no laughter, no youth, at Gómez Cardeña.

Nearby was the photo of a pretty young horsewoman, a South American girl, Amina Assís, who had come to him a year ago to study the science of fighting bulls from horseback. She had brightened the ranch considerably, and how he looked forward to her visits. He had been fond of her—not in love with her—and flattered by her interest and company. Here was someone he could teach and help. But now she had left him, too. Everything, everyone, seemed to have left him, and he was of no use to anyone.

On the coffee table was a copy of *Ferdinand the Bull,* a present from an American diplomat. But there was nothing else about bullfighting in the room except a painting by Spain's great artist, Zuloaga. Next to the fireplace the big oil hung, showing the young Belmonte striding across the ring—Belmonte, the man who invented modern bullfighting; Belmonte, the overcomer of insurmountable obstacles; Belmonte, the hero of the handicapped; Belmonte, the uncrowned king of Spain and Latin America; Belmonte, with his wolf jaw out disdainfully and blood running down his wounded leg.

Now he sat down in front of the little table by the bookshelves. He wrote a brief line: "No one is to be blamed for my death—Juan."

How long had this moment been in preparation? How many days, weeks, or years had it been in the making? In one of the books on the bookshelf near him was Camus' description of suicide preparing itself "like a work of art, secretly in the heart," without the artist's being aware of the process.

Before he shoved his right hand into the pocket of his bathrobe, before his fingers closed around the butt of the little 6.35 millimeter pistol, did he look up at the portrait? Did he think back to that day, when his leg was bleeding and twenty-four thousand people were screaming their love for him?

Or, did his thoughts go back to when love had ceased for him, when he was a dirty, little, ugly, stammering street urchin in Sevilla? Maybe he thought back to the terrible day when he was eight years old, when they told him his mother had died.

With the explosion of that pistol the last vestige of the golden era of bullfighting ended. The front pages of the newspapers held little else for days. The people of Sevilla gave their greatest hero a huge funeral, and thousands followed him through the streets. He was carried on their shoulders to the bullring for the last time, then to the cemetery, where he was buried next to the statue of Joselito.

All Spain cried inwardly at its loss, and during the next weeks, everyone speculated over one burning question: *Why had he done it?*

The night before he had remarked with some humor to a friend of mine, "There are only three things in life that I still like to do—make love, ride horses, and fight bulls. And my doctor has forbidden me all of them. I should like to die doing one of those things."

The same friend recalled seeing Belmonte the year before, the day after Hemingway committed suicide.

"Isn't that terrible?" remarked the friend.

"Not at all," said Belmonte calmly. "The glories were past for him. It was time."

Many Spanish Catholics voiced criticism of his suicide. But most people understood how it was for a man as great and complicated as Juan Belmonte and admired his courage.

"He was the most courageous man who ever lived," said a friend. "Death was the last bull of his life, and he was no more afraid of it than he was of any of the others."

The only member of my family who regularly came into El Matador was my brother, Hunt. Older than me by six years, he taught me to like San Francisco saloons long before I was legally allowed to drink in any. Earlier, I casually mentioned that he had a wooden leg, but believe me, there was nothing casual about his losing that leg.

Freud said there was no such thing as an accident, but then Freud never met my brother. Hunt was like humorist Don Marquis's character who "ran into accidents that started out to happen to somebody else."

Hunt was a boy wonder on a horse, and once when he was twelve, our father put him in an important horse show in San Mateo, California. The splendid horse, Pilot, was huge, my brother was small, and they were up against adults in the jumping competition. Hunt guided the horse skillfully into the first jump, and Pilot took it easily. The next jump came, and the next, and then Pilot arrived at the fence of the arena and took that, too. Then, with the bit in his teeth, he kept running until he was out of the grandstand, onto the highway, and down the highway, with Hunt standing in the stirrups and pulling the reins as hard as he could, unable to slow Pilot down as he ran between the cars for two miles. Somehow, horse and rider returned unscathed.

But a year later, Hunt's horse fell on him as he was performing the sack race in a gymkhana, at the Cate School, and he broke his hip. Then he broke his jaw and his wrist playing soccer. He was considered quite wild. I remember the first time he got drunk. Hunt was out on the town with his friend Ting-Ling Wergler and some older boys, and he tried to match their beer intake and couldn't. In his new car on the way home, the driver, Ting-Ling kept saying, "Now Hunt, when you feel yourself getting sick, stick your head through the window."

Hunt, semi-comatose, managed to keep it down until they reached our house. Ting-Ling helped him out of the car and up to the front door, but suddenly Hunt said, "Gonna be sick." He broke away from Ting-Ling, ran back to the car, stuck his head through the window, and threw up.

About this time, our father suffered a riding accident from which he never quite recovered, and after which our family became somewhat disarrayed. Hunt took to strong drink with a vengeance and for about two years he was a terror. He got his driver's license and began having automobile accidents—quite a few of them. Then his life changed abruptly, perhaps proving Dr. Freud right—there are no accidents.

When he was sixteen, Hunt entered a rodeo in Livingston, Montana, where he was working as a summer wrangler. In a terrible accident, his leg was crushed between two horses. Then he languished in the Livingston hospital for three months with blood poisoning. The Indian chief Max Big Man, a veteran of Custer's last stand, and Will James, the author of *Smoky the Cowhorse*, visited him. As his condition grew worse, he was moved to a San Francisco hospital, where he remained for almost two years. His leg was finally amputated at the knee.

But during the whole long painful ordeal he was an inspiration. I never heard him complain even once. Fitted with an artificial leg, he enrolled in Stanford, where he earned straight A's. He then got a job in Peru with a large American fish export company. He learned to do almost anything on his artificial leg—fish, hunt, ride, and fly a plane. He even won Lima's golf tournament one year. He never lost his sense of humor, and he was quick to poke fun at himself. "How many people do you know who go to Brooks Brothers and order one garter and a thumb tack?" He was a wonderful after-dinner speaker, and when called upon he would start out: "As I arise to my foot, it gives me great pleasure ... " and so on. His became a quiet life, but he had one last inadvertent adventure.

Over the years in Lima, he saw a great many corridas and met a lot of toreros, including Manolete and Arruza. So when in 1947, as a portly, thirty-year-old businessman, he decided to visit Spain, he made a special point of going to Sevilla to visit Juan Belmonte on his ranch. When I wrote Belmonte saying that Hunt would be calling on him, I merely said that he was as interested in *los toros* as

I; Belmonte mistakenly assumed that he was as interested in *fighting* them. He met Hunt at the door of his big ranch house, welcomed him warmly, and led him into the living room.

"I have arranged a little exhibition in your honor," he said.

"Who's fighting?" Hunt asked.

"Alvaro Domecq and myself," said Belmonte. "And you."

Hunt had never faced a fighting animal, and never expected to. Since he has only a slight limp, Belmonte had no idea he was dealing with a one-legged man. He just wanted to do right by a guest, my brother.

Hunt walked out on the porch, saw the bullring, the audience, and the corrals, where three respectably sized heifers were waiting. A butler was passing sherry to the dozen or so guests, and Hunt swept two glasses off the tray and downed them in quick succession. He managed to sneak a third while the *rejoneador,* Domecq, on his white *jerezano,* demonstrated his superb horsemanship, dodging and serpentining around a heifer while simulating placing banderillas in the Portuguese style. Then Don Juan himself went down into the arena, and even at fifty-five, he was all control and grace when he opened his cape in his unique verónica and the guests cheered. Belmonte came back up to the porch flushed and pleased that he was still able to perform the art form he himself had invented.

"*Ahora, amigo,*" Don Juan said, clapping Hunt on the shoulder. "It is your turn." As they went down the stairs to the little ring, Hunt cleared his throat and said hoarsely, "Don Juan, I guess you've seen a lot of people fight for the first time."

"*Sí,*" acknowledged Belmonte dryly, "*y por la última también.* And for the last as well."

The gate clanged open, the heifer galloped in and charged hard at the padded side of the picador's horse, its horns digging into the *peto,* its back legs driving even as the picador pricked its shoulders with his lance.

"Thank God it's not a big one," said Hunt.

"Same size as the one that killed Joselito," said Belmonte.

A young matador lured the animal away and left it standing in the middle of the arena, its flanks heaving in anger, its tail switching as it looked around for something to charge. Behind the protective *burladero* shield, Belmonte showed Hunt how to hold the muleta and spread it with the sword. Then he pointed at a place about twenty feet from the heifer.

"Now," he said, "over there."

Hunt stepped out from the *burladero.* He stood straight and tried to walk like Manolete. "If I'm going to get it," he was saying to himself, "I'm going to go out like Manolete!"

The heifer charged and Hunt froze, his eyes half closed, holding the muleta in the *pase de la muerte* position. Swoosh—it hurtled by, the horns missing his legs by a yard.

"It works!" Hunt exclaimed. "It actually wo—"

He never finished the sentence. The animal had wheeled tightly, and its blunt left horn struck him a glancing blow in the midsection.

Hunt managed two more passes, but he got turned around and tried to make the heifer pass between himself and the fence, usually a bad move. The heifer drove a horn into his leg, luckily, the wooden one. Belmonte stepped into the ring in a flash, shoved his cape in the animal's face, and lured the heifer away from the fallen man.

Hunt got up mad and frustrated. This time, when the animal charged, he decided to show the critter an old Montana trick. Tossing away the muleta, he grabbed the attacking heifer by the off horn with one hand and by the snout with the other. Wrenching its neck and falling backward, he neatly bulldogged, or cowdogged, the *vaca brava* for the first time in Spain's history. Belmonte, who thought he'd seen everything that could happen in a bull-ring, scratched his head as he walked over to where my grinning brother held the animal helpless.

"*Ya está muerta?*" the great matador asked between amazement and amusement. "Is it dead yet?"

John Fulton was in his late teens when he came into El Matador, the first matador to enter our saloon. But he was and is different—he is a professional American bullfighter. Handsome, charming, and talented in many ways, he has had an extraordinary career. After seeing the film *Blood and Sand,* this seventeen-year-old Phila-delphia boy abruptly decided to go to Mexico and become a matador. This is somewhat like seeing the film *The Red Shoes* and declaring: I will go to Russia and become a star at the Bolshoi. He wrote me a letter saying he was deter-mined to achieve his goal of becoming a full matador. I told him it was a hopeless dream and to quit before he even started. He ignored my counsel and went first to Mexico to study the grueling science of tauromachy. Then he went on to Spain and studied with the great Juan Belmonte. Success took years of hard struggle, but he made it, and he is the only American to become a senior matador, having been given the *alternativa* ceremony in both the Sevilla and Madrid arenas. Considering the phys-ical dangers, the political chicanery, and the peer jealousy of the taurine world, it would probably have been easier for him to have become an astronaut. Incredibly, he has only suffered one terrible goring, and he is still fighting bulls, and doing it well. When he is not out with the bulls, he is in his Sevilla studio painting them; he is an accomplished artist and has illustrated several books, his latest, in 1994, a James Michener book entitled *Miracle in Sevilla.*

Once one Sunday in the Maestranza of Sevilla, perhaps the most prestigious arena in the world, he had a bad afternoon, as any performer can have. He'd been injured a few days before, he'd taken the fight on short notice, and the bulls were wild and totally unmanageable. But the public accepts no excuses, and he was jeered roundly. John's manager took him out to dinner afterward to help him forget the disaster.

As he brought the menus, the waiter sneered, "Hombre, did they ever boo you today! *Caray,* did they throw things and boo you today!"

The manager reached up, grabbed the waiter by the collar, yanked his head down to table level, and said, "Listen, you son of the great whore, let me tell you something very basic: They will never, never boo a waiter!"

I think everyone in the arts should remind themselves from time to time of that important thought: No one will ever boo a critic. As Theodore Roosevelt wrote so long ago:

> It is not the critic who counts,
> Nor the man who points out
> how the strong man stumbles,
> or where the doer of deeds
> could have done better.
> The credit belongs to the man
> who is actually in the arena;
> whose face is marred by dust and sweat;
> who strives valiantly;
> who errs and may fail again . . .
> so that his place shall never be
> with those cold and timid souls
> who know neither victory nor defeat.

An amazing afternote to the Fulton saga: in Mexico, on April 2, 1994, John appeared for one last fight in the San Miguel de Allende arena, where he'd fought for the first time almost four decades before. In front of 3,000 people, he performed brilliantly with his second bull, killed the animal with a perfect thrust, and was awarded both ears. At the age of sixty-two, he became the oldest matador to appear in a regulation corrida. As he was carried out of the ring by the crowd in triumph, he shouted at me, "What do I do for an encore?" I replied, "Nothing, I hope!"

His son cut off his father's pigtail in the traditional emotional ceremony that signifies that the matador will never fight again. But with toreros, one never knows. As Conchita Cintrón, the great matadora of yesteryear, wrote me: "I dare say John is now deep in satisfaction. But he is mistaken; nobody who has belonged to the arenas can leave them; the rings have magic and nobody says farewell to them . . . "

I began to notice that a very pretty, fortyish woman kept coming into the Matador on a regular basis. She would sit alone at the piano bar sipping a grasshopper and ask pianist Johnny Cooper to play songs like "Sweet Lorraine" and "My Funny Valentine." She had beautiful long red hair, white skin, and amazing deep-set eyes.

I felt I knew her, yet I also knew that we had never met. One night, exercising my *droit de seigneur* as the boniface, I introduced myself. Her name was Virginia Lewis, she was newly arrived in San Francisco, and she was an interior decorator. In the ensuing conversation, it turned out she was the daughter of Dr. Claude Lewis, Sinclair Lewis's older brother. Once I knew that, I could see why she looked familiar: she had her uncle's high forehead, his red hair, and his penetrating, pale blue eyes. The resemblance was hard to fathom, however, for he was ugly and she was beautiful. I showed her the portrait I had done of him, the one shown on page 186 (which is now at the University of Texas in Austin).

We talked all that night and the next night as well about that enigmatic man, who for five short (and long) months was the principal figure in my life and whose presence stays with me vividly to this day.

When I met the legendary author in 1947, he had been on the wagon for eight years, the longest period of sobriety in his adult life. It was not to last.

That year, at age twenty-five, I had returned home from four years in the Consular Corps and from bullfighting in Spain and Peru. While visiting my parents in Santa Barbara, California, I read that Sinclair Lewis was in town for a few weeks. I figured we had a lot in common, since I'd read all his books and he'd read all his books. Also, my agent, Marcella Powers, was his ex-mistress. I wrote him a note asking if I could meet him. Probably the most famous and wealthiest novelist in the world, he was also America's first Nobel Prize winner for literature, so I was surprised and elated when he invited me to tea. He asked to read the first seventy-five pages of the novel I was working on, and the next day he advised me to throw away the first seventy-two pages. He asked for the next seventy-five, called me at two in the morning to say he liked them, and offered me a job as secretary-companion at his home in Massachusetts "as soon as you learn how to play chess."

This was a bittersweet time for the author of such landmarks as *Main Street, Babbitt, Arrowsmith,* and *Elmer Gantry.* On the one hand, his beloved twenty-seven-year-old mistress of ten years, Marcella, had left him; on the other, he was anticipating great things from his new novel, *Kingsblood Royal.* This is the story of a respected small-town banker who is reviled and ostracized by his

"First of the Day"
Sinclair Lewis at Williamstown, Mass.
Barnaby Conrad

fellow citizens when it is disclosed that he has "Negro blood" in his background. Well researched and passionately felt, it was one of the first books to make a plea for understanding the plight of blacks in America.

Less than a month later, I flew to New York and took the morning train to Williamstown, Massachusetts. Mr. Lewis met me at the station with Joseph, his dignified black chauffeur.

People who knew him intimately called him "Hal." People who knew him well called him "Red." People who knew him slightly called him "Sinclair." I called him "Mr.

Lewis." I was excited and a little apprehensive, but he was in an expansive mood and put me at ease immediately.

"Let's get home now and find out how you do against the old Red Chess Master."

He was an awesome and startling sight. At sixty-two, he was tall and fiercely ugly, quite the ugliest person I had ever seen. I recoiled from the haunted, sunken eyes and his scarlet face, which was ravaged and scarred, pocked and cratered from countless operations for skin cancer. His once-blazing red hair was now thin and orangy-white.

Yet when he started to talk I no longer thought him ugly. He was kind and rapacious, charming and witty, factual and fanciful; he was reverent and irreverent, gossipy and profound. One no longer was aware of a face but only of a powerful personality and a towering imagination and great boyish enthusiasm. We talked of all manner of things. I learned later that this was a talking period for him, a lonely period. Subsequently, I would know his long silent times; both were equally compulsive.

He talked about everyone in the old days, all his friends, from Robert Benchley to Edna St. Vincent Millay to H. L. Mencken to George Bernard Shaw. But he also talked about the present and the future. He was very excited about *Kingsblood Royal.*

As Joseph drove us in the convertible Buick sedan through the town and through Williams College, Mr. Lewis pumped me for information about Marcella.

"Does she seem happy? Happy with that Boy Scout?"

I said, "Yes, very," and saw a look of wistful pain cross his face.

"They're always happy in the beginning," he muttered. "But you wait. Hell, if you can't be happy in the first month, you're in trouble. Funny, I left my first wife when I was forty-two. Left my second when I was fifty-two. And now this ungrateful girl ups and leaves me when I'm sixty-two for one of the Rover Boys!"

"Mr. Lewis," I asked, "just what are my duties? I'm not really qualified to be a secretary."

"Your duties," he said, "are to get up every morning at five-thirty and work on that goddamn book of yours!"

Four and a half miles in back of Williamstown on Oblong Road, the seven hundred and fifty acres of fields, mountains, and woods of Thorvale Farm began. Mr. Lewis proudly showed me around the beautiful estate, which was complete with a trout stream, a purposefully rustic swimming pool set in a birch glen, guest houses, barns, and a tennis court. The handsome manor house, with a fine view of Mount Greylock, had seven bedrooms and five baths, and was carefully furnished. Bookcases were everywhere, even running up the stairs. Where there weren't books, there were paintings by the American impressionist Childe Hassam.

It looked as though he had always been in this house and would stay forever. But in fact, he had been in the place little more than a year, and the restless Mr. Lewis would put the house up for sale a year later, resuming his lonely journey in search of a happiness he would never find.

That night I played chess with Mr. Lewis before dinner. I had studied chess for only a few weeks and had little talent for the game, but I managed to maneuver his king into a bad position fairly soon. I left to go to the bathroom, and when I returned, I could swear the pieces had been moved to my disadvantage. But I didn't say anything, and I managed to win anyway. He seemed upset.

"Luck," he snarled, "sheer luck!"

Then I remembered Marcella's admonition: "You mustn't win at chess—not too often, anyway. It's the most important thing in his day. Especially now that he's 'with book' and very testy."

He was a trifle sullen at dinner, I thought, frowning over the fine leg of lamb that Joseph had cooked and served. For a fastidious man, he had infantile table manners: he liked to swirl his mashed potatoes and peas and meat and a butter ball and bits of bread all together in a Charybdis-like concentric swirl. Then he sent back the plate to the kitchen, the food half-eaten and covered with a film of cigarette ashes like some meal interrupted at the time of the Pompeian disaster. He had barely eaten half his dessert when he said, "Now my friend, we'll see how much beginner's luck was involved in that first game!"

I followed him out of the living room and waited while he fortified himself by eating several chocolates. (There was always a box of Whitman's Samplers in every room, most of the contents ruined for anyone else by Mr. Lewis's inquiring forefinger.) He sat down at the chess table and rubbed his hands with anticipation. He immediately set out to lure me into a fool's mate, to beat me in a minimum of moves. Though it was one of the first maneuvers my instructor had showed me how to avoid, I let myself fall into the trap.

"Ah hah!" he exulted. "That will show you!"

He was delighted and ate three chocolates in celebration. In a euphoric mood, he bid me goodnight.

"Welcome to Thorvale—see you bright and early!" he said, as he went up the stairs, breaking wind triumphantly with every step.

I woke up the next morning before the alarm went off at five-thirty. It was still dark as I dressed and went downstairs.

He was ahead of me. I saw him—Ichabod Crane—sitting in the dining room in a faded brown bathrobe, hunched over a cup of coffee. His three false front teeth weren't in place yet, which did not enhance his appearance. He wore a green eyeshade, like a small-town newspaper editor, and his orangy hair shot out from the sides of his head like horns. He pointed with a trembling finger at a thermos and a cup at the other end of the table. I sat down and poured a cup of coffee. It was quiet for a while except for Mr. Lewis's slurping of coffee and the keening of the quail outside. Smoking steadily, he stared off into space as though fascinated by a moving picture visible to his eyes alone. I finished my coffee, and he still hadn't spoken. I noticed he had Band-Aids on his fingers, which meant he was working, for he was a hunt-and-peck typist and had sensitive fingers. The backs of his skeletal hands were foxed like an antique manuscript.

Finally, he said, "I'm intolerable in the morning. I get bearable around noon, and around six o'clock I'm quite a splendid chap."

I noticed his breath smelled like photographic negatives.

I went back to my studio and worked until I heard the breakfast chimes at eight-thirty. After breakfast, we both went back to our work. When the mail arrived at eleven, Mr. Lewis came into my studio and handed me several fan letters and requests for autographs.

"Here," he said, "play Sinclair Lewis and answer these. Say anything you want and sign my signature to them." Then he tore open and read another letter.

"Look what this sonovabitch wants!"

He handed it to me. It was from an attorney, and it read:

Dear Lewis:
   Have read some of your works and would like to ask a few favors. Please send me a list of your stories, your autograph, your picture, and a letter describing your life. How many children you have and their names.
   Thanking you I am,
                                        Yours truly,
                                        James J. Sneath

"I think I'll answer this bastard myself," said Mr. Lewis, and the gleam of battle was in his pale eyes. "Barny, take a letter!"

Though I knew no shorthand, I managed to keep up with his exaggeratedly polite tone. He dictated as though conversing pleasantly to his new pen pal:

My dear Jimmy:

There was only one thing about your letter that I didn't like. It was so sort of formal. True, we have never met, and somehow I feel we are not likely to, but isn't this a democratic country? So let me call you Jim and you call me Skinny or any other friendly name. No, Jim, I haven't got a photograph of me here, but I'll run right down and have one taken. I'm preparing a letter about my life for you, but it's been a pretty long one and a pretty bad one. That'll take me several weeks. Meantime, Jimmy, I'm interested in lawyers. Kindly send me your photo, pictures of your home, your office, a list of your assets and liabilities, average income, and the books you've read since 1930, if any. Kindly inform me whether you've ever defended a bootlegger or an author, and why. How do you get along with your wife? Kindly explain the sex part in detail.

Yours affectionately,

Sinclair Lewis

Another reply he wrote began so wonderfully: "Dear John: How unwise of you to hate me. . . . " I had great fun becoming Sinclair Lewis for two hours or so a day, answering the fan mail. He would enjoy reading my replies and would chuckle over some. "God, I write a good letter!" he'd say sometimes, pleased. Often he would correct or add to them, and I learned from it.

My actual secretarial duties were few. I used to cut the vast lawns with a power mower after lunch and go trout fishing in the stream. Sometimes I would go pick up books for Mr. Lewis at the library and meet visitors at the train. Every few days I would drive down to the bank to deposit ten or fifteen pages of his new novel, *The God Seeker*, in a vault; it made sense, a Sinclair Lewis novel being worth hundreds of thousands of dollars.

I was overwhelmed by the guests who would come to see Sinclair Lewis, by the conversations I was privy to. Once George Jean Nathan, the curmudgeonly New York drama critic and partner of H. L. Mencken in the famous *Mercury* magazine, came to spend a weekend. He brought along the willowy actress Julie Haydon, his great and good companion for seventeen years. At one point, I naively asked him if he and Miss Haydon were engaged.

"*Engaged?*" he said, and the way he gargled the word made it sound four-lettered. "*Engaged* to be *married* you mean? Listen, my boy, and take heed: the concept of marriage is just as though someone were to take a liking to a particular brand of beer, and then announced to the world, I like this beer, it is a great beer, I shall now quit my job and go to work for the brewery!"

Later the biographer Carl Van Doren and Sinclair Lewis were talking after George and the pallid and ethereal Julie had left the living room.

"What do you think, Red?" Carl asked. "Is George really in love with Julie?"

"No," said Lewis, "I think he's just a necrophiliac who's too lazy to dig."

I felt it was all too good to be true for a young ambitious writer like myself, and it was.

On August 29, Mr. Lewis abruptly told me that he would be leaving for the Midwest in five days, would be closing the house, and that I was no longer needed. I was fired, and I did not learn the reason for many years. I thought we got along so well—what had I done?

He accompanied me to the station. Red—I could only bring myself to call him by that undignified nickname now that I was no longer in his employ—was warm and lavish with great predictions for my novel, *The Innocent Villa*, and full of fatherly admonitions. As we said good-bye, he awkwardly handed me a first edition of *Cass Timberlane*. It was inscribed: "To Barny Conrad, whom a summer at Thorvale has proved the most amiable man living."

I was sad and bewildered as the train pulled out, leaving his pathetic silhouette hunched and alone on the platform.

I had several letters from Sinclair Lewis, some warm and encouraging, others cold and cutting, depending upon his mood. One merely said, "I take it that, this winter, you have decided that you are not going to be a writer—not at all. Your decision, or at least hankering, to flee off to the bogus paradises of Paris and Naples after a winter devoted to aimless idleness, is the old story. That your decision is unconscious probably makes it only the more final."

I did not see him again until 1949 when I went to France on my honeymoon.

I heard that he was in Paris, and I called him. He insisted that my wife, Dale, and I have dinner with him. We picked him up at his hotel. He'd only been in Paris a day, but he seemed jubilant, frenetically so. He was stimulated by the city he'd known during his early triumphs.

"First time I've really been in Paris for twenty years," he said. "I'm going to take you to a marvelous little place on the Left Bank where we all used to go. You'll love it— gay, stimulating—all the good artists, writers go there, the top newspapermen, the thinkers."

We crossed the river and, after asking a few people, arrived at the address. It was a miserable and dirty little café, with only one customer, a student who was studying a book by the light of a candle in a bottle.

"This can't be the place!" Red exclaimed.

Dale checked the address and the name, and it was correct.

We sat down at a table, and Red ordered a drink. I had never seen him drink before. It was astonishing to watch him down a brandy; it disappeared with a single sucking sound. He had three to our one and kept looking around the dusty café, frowning deeply.

"This is simply not the place," he repeated irritably. "That's all there is to it. The other place was far bigger— brightly lit, music, full of people. Not it at all."

As we ate our depressing meal, the waiter, as a matter of routine, brought over an old ledger that served as a guest book. It was full of names of the past. On almost the first yellowed page I saw the signatures: John Dos Passos, Dorothy Thompson, Sinclair Lewis. I tried to show the page to Red, but he wouldn't look at it.

"Matter of fact," he said as he motioned the waiter for another brandy, "I remember now—wasn't even on this street. Different part of town."

Somehow we got into a discussion with the student. Red invited him over and asked him a great many questions about his life and studies. The student didn't introduce himself and neither did we. He spoke English well but with a thick accent. He was a literature major and was very serious behind his thick glasses.

"And what American writers do you read?" Red asked, too casually.

The student thought for a moment, then said, "My favorites are Fitzgerald, Hemingway, Steinbeck, and Sinclair . . . "

Red's face lit up pathetically. "Ah, Sinclair . . . "

"Upton Sinclair," continued the youth.

Red frowned and cleared his throat uncomfortably. "Any others?"

The youth shrugged. "I've read them all. But those are the ones I most admire."

We left. In the taxi, Red mimicked the student's accent and manner to perfection: "My fahvoreets ahr Feetzgerohl, Emeenwhy, Stynabecque, an,"—here he departed slightly from the original—"An, thees Seenclair, thees Seenclair Loowees."

Though I found it hard to believe, it was as though he had actually convinced himself that the youth had listed his name among his favorites. And that evening when we joined Red's brother, Claude, at the Café du Dome, Red recounted the story, the accent honed, complete with embellishments. ("My favoreet nohvell off theese Seenclair Loowees ees how-you-call-heem, *Ahrohsmeet.*")

He had several more brandies, and then we helped Claude get him home in a cab and up the stairs to the lobby of the hotel.

"If he keeps drinking like this he'll be dead in a year," said Claude mournfully, as we said good night at the elevator.

Claude's sad prediction did not miss by much, for Sinclair Lewis died in Rome of alcoholism the following year. I heard of a final macabre irony: A friend of mine went into the United States Embassy at Rome and saw a consular official down on her knees with a broom and pan. "What are you doing?" he asked her. "Sweeping up Sinclair Lewis," was the answer. Red's ashes had been put in a safe pending final disposal, and the urn had fallen out, its contents spilled.

Many years later, in the Matador, Virginia Lewis asked, "He was so fond of you—why did you get fired?"

I couldn't answer that. Today I know. *Cherchez la femme.*

It started one morning in Williamstown when I went down to get a book for Mr. Lewis from Washburne's book shop with his admonition, "Be sure you're here for lunch at twelve sharp!" ringing in my ears. Behind the counter was a petite lady of about twenty-six. We got to talking about books and movies and fishing and Sinclair Lewis and other things. Her name was Ida Kay, and she was tan and pretty. As we chatted, I realized in a rush what a monastic life I had been leading the past few months. My youthful ego delighted at being the center of attention for a change. Suddenly, I looked at my watch and realized I only had eight minutes to get home for lunch. Blurting out, "See you tomorrow!" I dashed out of the store and jumped into the parked car, but for some reason neither of the keys would go into the ignition. I tried every way to force them, to no avail. Finally, in desperation, I took off the hand brake and let the car coast down the inclined main street until I came to a garage. I explained I was in a great hurry, that something was wrong with the ignition, and then went to phone Joseph to tell Mr. Lewis that I would be unavoidably delayed. When I returned, a mechanic was lying under the steering wheel working away on the ignition.

"Say, whose car is this anyway?" he asked as he hammered.

"Sinclair Lewis's," I said.

The man stopped working. "This isn't Mr. Lewis's car," he said. "He has a Buick."

And indeed it wasn't. In my foggy state, I had picked someone else's vehicle. I phoned the police to say if anyone reported a missing car, it was in this garage. Then I abashedly apologized to the garageman, ran back up the street, collected the correct automobile, and sped home.

I quelled some of Mr. Lewis's wrath at my tardiness by telling him about the lovely girl at the bookstore.

"Ask her to lunch tomorrow," he said unexpectedly. "She sounds like Marcella."

Ida came—that day and many subsequent ones—and Mr. Lewis was delighted with her. Unfortunately, so was I, and when I would go walking by the stream with her or would take her to a college play or to the movies, we would find Mr. Lewis waiting up for us and scowling like an overly protective father. Mark Schorer, in his monumental biography *Sinclair Lewis,* wrote that Lewis

  . . . was indebted to Barnaby Conrad . . . for introducing
  him to another companion who was to be of real com-

fort to him before he abandoned Williamstown—
a young woman named Ida Kay who clerked in the
college bookstore—pretty, sprightly, literate, free to be
called upon at any time, full of chatter and gossip and
sufficient deference to the mighty to prove highly
satisfactory.

It was more than Schorer knew. Not long ago I had a
letter from Ida. She was dying of cancer and wanted to tell
me how much our brief affair had meant to her. Red, she
said, had fired me to get me out of the way; he had fallen
in love with her, and she had made him forget Marcella.
He offered her the moon. He took her to Europe with him,
and despite the vast difference in their ages, he asked her
to marry him. But she returned to Williamstown and happily married a young college professor.

Ida's tale revealed another sad chapter in the life of
our illustrious novelist, proving once again Fitzgerald's
dictum, "Nothing fails like success."

Sinclair Lewis died in 1951, and so he never knew of
my novel *Matador,* and he never graced my saloon with
his mercurial presence. *Menos mal,* as the Spaniards say,
just as well. His niece, Virginia, agreed with me: he would
have looked around, perhaps enjoyed himself briefly, and
then, before lurching out of the swinging doors, he would
have snarled, "Anything to keep from writing, eh Barny?
Get back to that damned typewriter!"

When I did get back to the typewriter to write another
novel, finally, it was called *Dangerfield,* and it was based
completely upon Sinclair Lewis. Though I'm sure he
wouldn't have admitted it, the picture of the aging, lonely
novelist was accurate and affectionate, and I think he
might even have basked a little in the book's success, for it
got good reviews and was later made into a Broadway
play.

I was becoming increasingly bored with North Beach nightlife; not all the nights in El Matador were exciting ones. One night my manager, Niels Mortensen, suggested that to while away the boredom we write a novel together. I'd read in the newspaper that 57,000 acres of oil-rich land in Southern California was set aside for the California condors, whose population then numbered forty-nine.

"How about if a bunch of bad guys are hired by an oil company to kill the condors."

"And our hero, a naturalist, has to try to stop them," Niels said, enthusiastically.

Niels was much more than the manager of a nightclub: he'd been a bronc buster in Montana, a ski instructor in Vermont, a prize-winning reporter in Chicago, and a freelance writer for such magazines as *True* and *Esquire.* He had a fine imagination. For example, it was he who invented the piano bar and the blackboard in the men's room, and he who set out on our tables little cardboard tents that read: "A cover charge of ten cents will be levied in order to keep out the riff-raff."

We set to work on the book with a will, even though Evelyn Waugh once wrote that the idea of two people writing a book is like three people getting together to make a baby.

Over the months during the slow hours at the saloon, we wrote the book, *Forty-Nine Ugly Birds,* and had fun doing it. A New York publisher took it, gave us a good advance, and changed the title to *Endangered.*

"Now we need a smashing blurb for the jacket," said our editor, "from someone famous."

Niels asked me if I didn't know William F. Buckley, Jr. I said that at Yale I had known his brother, who kept a boa constrictor named Martha that he fed white mice to every other Thursday in a cocktail ceremony, but that I'd only met the formidable Mr. W. F. Buckley, Jr., twice—once very briefly at a restaurant and once when he came into the Matador.

"Write him!" said Niels.

I protested that he was so busy, that I didn't want to bother him, and we'd never hear from him, but Niels insisted.

I took a deep breath and sat down at the typewriter. If I was going to get Buckley's attention, it couldn't be your ordinary plea for a blurb; he must receive those by the dozens. I came up with the following and sent it off with a copy of the novel.

Dear Bill:

I'm enclosing a novel, *Endangered,* that a friend of mine and I have just finished and which Putnam's plans to publish this spring. If, in spite of your horrendous schedule, you could find time to read it and perhaps say something not unkind about it, that would be enormously pleasing. Tolstoy it is not, but a light summer read in a hammock it may quite possibly be.

If you find yourself too busy, you're too busy, and don't give it another thought.

Do not for a moment feel guilty about the matter or dwell on the many favors I've done you over the years. Such as the blurb that I gave you for your recent little Sea Scout Manual or, going back a bit, the money I lent you as a rather threadbare though promising undergraduate at college. Or the fact that I was the first to spot the worth of your first book, *God and Man at Yale,* and saw it through to publication at Vantage Press.

Or that I introduced you to both the works of G. K. Chesterton and the girl who would subsequently become your wife, got you "in good" with C. B. Luce, personally gave your dog Rowley his first gentle worming, put up with your brother Jim's boa constrictor and his political views, both equally convoluted, honed your spindly vocabulary, formed your tiny left hand around its first tenth on the harpsichord, physically protected you in the studio from the smoldering violence of Gore Vidal, encouraged your first fumbling attempts at navigation ("Buckley, goddammit, leave the moon out of it altogether!"), and, of course, managed to keep you a member of the Bohemian Club when the elders wanted you sent down for buggery.

No—do not give any of the above a moment's thought; if you are too busy, I understand and that is that.

And know that if you decide you cannot do this that I shall never think twice about it, and that I shall always remain your fervent, your true, and your loyal acquaintance.

Sincerely,
Barnaby Conrad

To our amazement and delight, Mr. Buckley immediately wired:

Dear Barnaby:

Your book is great! Exciting, dramatic, sensual, gripping, moving, hilarious! You may quote me!

Bill

Of course, Mr. Buckley probably never even read the book, and there certainly was nothing hilarious (at least intentionally) about the novel—but don't worry, we used the quote on that dust jacket!

Some time later, Bill invited me to be on his TV program "The Firing Line." The subject was "Bullfighting: Art or Butchery?" As we taped the rather leaden hour in a New York studio one afternoon, I noticed Muhammad Ali sitting restlessly in the small audience, and after my stint, he was interviewed by Buckley for a separate segment. It was a brilliant performance, the heavyweight champion slugging it out verbally with the erudite Buckley and winning most of the rounds.

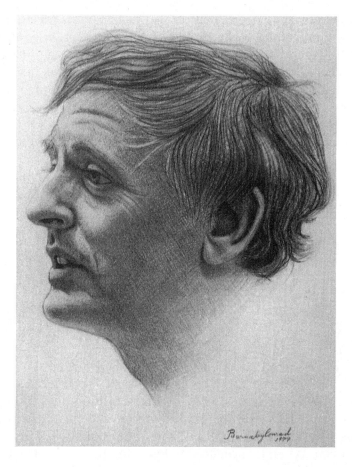

Buckley introduced me to the huge man afterward, and I said how fine I thought the interview had been.

"Well, it *did* go rather well," Ali said quietly. "They said I was up there for a whole hour." He snapped his fingers. "It seemed to go just like that. Now when *you* were up there, it seemed to take *forever!*"

Since then I have seen Bill many times and have great admiration for him. I have a friend who said, "He looks so damned arrogant, so cold, so detached, always looks like a man holding the leash of a defecating dog."

Quite apart from matters political, I wish my friend could meet him away from a camera or a press conference. He is polite, always a gentleman, generous, amusing, modest, and yes, warm. I am amazed at his productivity and his versatility. Apart from his column and TV and *National Review* obligations, he finds time to paint, ski, sail the Atlantic or Pacific oceans, write a book a year, be a good father and husband, and, of course, play his beloved harpsichord every day.

His humor is constant and unfailing, such as when it was rumored that he was to be named to an important post in President Reagan's cabinet. A reporter asked what his position would be, and Buckley said slyly, "That of ventriloquist, I presume."

When his niece Priscilla wanted to know why Bobby Kennedy had never accepted Buckley's offer to debate, he said, "Why does the baloney fear the slicer?"

I suppose what I admire most about Bill Buckley is his sense of faith. Not just in his God, but in humanity and our most important traits—intelligence, desire, charity, love, and, most of all, the ability to laugh at oneself.

The story of this charcoal portrait is this: I invited Buckley to the Santa Barbara Writers' Conference on short notice in 1977. To my amazement he accepted, dropped his frantic schedule, flew out, and made a dazzling speech. When he prepared to leave the next day, I tried to press an honorarium on him. Knowing the size of our tubercular budget, he declined. "Let me at least catch your airfare," I said. He shook his head. "This one's on me!"

How does one repay William F. Buckley, Jr.? I devised a plan of retaliation: At the Bohemian Club's summer encampment I snuck several candid photos of Buckley. Then I did this sketch from them and sent him the result. When he tried to pay me, I demurred, saying grandly, "*This* one's on me!"

But when Buckley's next book, *Airborne,* was published, I was sent a copy plus a large check, for instead of the author's photo on the jacket was my sketch of him!

Moral: Never try to best either Muhammad Ali or William F. Buckley, Jr., at their own game.

When I was introduced to the legendary actor Jimmy Stewart, he said in his gracious, diffident, charming drawl which sounded like a parody, "I've very much enjoyed your books, Mister Conrad."

"That, Mr. Stewart," I said, "is the worst imitation of Jimmy Stewart I have ever heard."

"I know," he said shaking his head abashedly. "I'm workin' on it, workin' on it."

The portrait shown here belongs to his daughter, and I am pleased because I think it's one of my best.

Herb Caen pops up throughout this book, as he has throughout my life. As the greatest San Francisco name dropper of them all, he was there at the beginning of El Matador and there at the end.

In his fifty-odd years as the *San Francisco Chronicle*'s premier columnist, Herb has celebrated the foibles, flights of fancy, and achievements of the city's citizens in a manner unrivaled except by Walter Winchell in New York. He has missed only one of his daily columns (because of illness) in all that time, a remarkable record by a remarkable man. He may be California's wittiest man, the Fred Astaire of three-dot journalism, the thinking man's gagmeister.

I met the already famous columnist at a debutante party in Hillsborough in 1940, a sad little affair, since

there was only one deb that year because of the impending war. We continued our friendship at Yale, where Herb
was in officer's training school for the Air Corps. After the
war, I found myself back in San Francisco trying to be a
writer, always with Herb's interest and support. No matter

how inept a book or article I wrote, Herb would give it a mention, even if his uncompromising standards would only allow him a plug of the "well, that *is* a baby" variety.

When I opened El Matador, Herb was the first in the door and was such a regular customer that we gave him his own table with a small brass plaque on it. Single-handedly, Herb made my saloon *the* place to go by recording the doings and sayings of the many celebrities who frequented the spot. Herb himself brought in such stars as Saroyan, André Previn, Sinatra, Capote, and John Huston. Worldly, sophisticated, well-read, and gregarious, he seems to know everyone in the world; he somehow makes them honorary San Franciscans, and daily lets us, his readers, have the privilege of knowing them, too.

Life in those days, officially known as the Good Old Days, seemed to center around the Prado, the Hungry i, Vanessi's, New Joe's, the Buena Vista, Jack's, Al William's Papagayo Room, Trader Vic's, and the Lower Mark bar. Enrico's was the place for action at lunch over endless rounds of "The Match Game," and what wonderful items came out of there. Herb always seems to be at the right place to catch the bon mot at the right time. In Normandy, for example, a few hours after the horrendous D-Day landings, he had to go to the bathroom. Approaching a quintessential old Frenchman in a smock and beret, he asked, "*Monsieur, s'il vous plait, où est le lavabo?*" The old man flung open his grateful arms and with tears in his eyes exclaimed, "*Mais, toute la belle France, mon ami, toute la belle France!*"

Not just San Francisco but all the world has been fodder for Herb's columns, from Paris to Cairo and London to China. No travel writer I know can make you *feel* a foreign place so quickly and in such telling detail. In 1959, Herb came to visit my wife and me in Tahiti, discovered snorkeling and a lovely island girl, and wrote six of his best articles about that then relatively unknown island. In Spain,

Herb and I went to the corrida in Malaga with Orson Welles, when the bull jumped the barrier and landed in Orson's copious lap. "The animal quickly realized its predicament and got back into the arena," reported Herb.

On a jaunt to Tijuana, we saw Dominguín put up a great display of skill and courage to an enthralled crowd. One woman got so carried away that as the handsome matador circled the arena in triumph she stood up and threw down her bra to him—an act that Herb later described as "an empty gesture if I ever saw one!" On our return airplane flight, Herb became curious about the little porcelain "Atomic Pig" he'd bought from a sidewalk vendor: all on its own, its ears wiggled and its tail wagged. Herb broke it open to learn the mystery, and five angry bees stormed out to the near-panic of the stewardesses and passengers. Another great column was born for us to enjoy over breakfast: "Bees in the afternoon."

While Herb is known for his "Chronicling" of the immediate and the quick, he is unequalled in his role as a writer of obituaries. His ability to capture the essence of a person's life in a few paragraphs was demonstrated superbly in a column dedicated to the complicated actor Sterling Hayden, as well as in his eulogies to Trader Vic, Mayor Moscone, Benny Goodman, William Saroyan, and dozens of others. He cares about these people and makes his readers care, too. In his later years, the feisty, prickly Sackamenna Kid has mellowed to a point where someone recently said of him, "He now wears life like a loose garment." But his writing has lost none of its bite or humor.

One of my regrets when it comes my time to shuffle off to the great match game in the sky will be that I won't be able to read Herb's write-up of my leave taking. Meanwhile, I intend to enjoy to the fullest my daily Caen fix, his diurnal paean to a great city for whose image he is almost single-handedly responsible.

El Fin del Matador

And whatever happened to El Matador? Whatever happened to that unique and wonderful place? For that matter, whatever happened to San Francisco?

The end of El Matador started with the street itself. In the 1960s Broadway went topless. Unlike those classy strippers, such as Norma Vincent Peel and Tempest Storm, who did their thing elegantly in the chaste style of Gypsy Rose Lee, girls wearing nothing but spangled G-strings "danced" in cannabis-drenched joints in front of glassy-eyed customers. After a while, even the G-strings were dispensed with. Soon a hamburger place opened across the street featuring nude waitresses. The sidewalk barkers for these places were offensively aggressive, driving as many people away from the street as they lured to it. The last straw was the Topless Shoe Shine Stand right next to Ferlinghetti's famed City Lights bookstore, where bovine ladies buffed shoes in the buff. Soon the last bastions of decency remaining on the grand old street began to leave: Vanessi's esteemed restaurant moved, Mike's Pool Hall closed, and the Bocce Ball, where the waiters and waitresses sang opera, folded. Even the fabled transvestite emporium, Finnochio's (where "Joe Finnochio lived off the labors of his fruits," as Herb Caen said), was offended and threatened to move to a nicer neighborhood.

My decision to sell the Matador was a rather abrupt one. It was mostly because of The Girl. For some years I'd been in a bad marriage, one that certainly hadn't been helped by the Matador's hours, demands, and temptations. I'd always fantasized that one evening The Girl would come in. Perhaps, subconsciously, that's the reason I created the spot in the first place: I had made a beautiful, elegant oasis where surely a beautiful, elegant woman would someday want to enter, and, by God, one fall day in 1961, she did, looking more beautiful and more elegant than I'd ever dared to hope.

Her name was Mary, and I remember she had brown, sun-streaked hair, a perky hat cocked over twinkly eyes, a full white blouse, and unbelievably long legs that disappeared—finally—under a plaid skirt. She was twenty-six, divorced with two children, and—to lapse into Jane Eyreese: Reader, we married. Not only was she beautiful, she became my secretary, my accountant, my traveling companion, and an imaginative cook (Julia Child is her cousin, which should tell you a lot about my present waistline).

And so it was that I decided to give up El Matador. It was a great place, but I'd had a long succession of smoky, ginny nights—I had books to write and paintings to paint which would emerge all the better for my not having rolled in past midnight the night before. Fun's fun, but I came to realize what Noel Coward once said: "Work is so much more fun than fun." The era was over, and so I said farewell to the Barbary Coast and amen to all of that.

Under the aegis of Australian John Clarke and Robert Catecchi, the Matador continued for a few years as a jazz club, hosting the likes of Cal Tjader, Brazil 66, Charlie Byrd, Laurindo Almeida, George Shearing, and Joe

Bushkin. I left all my stuff, the paintings, costumes, and the bull's head in place, but I took with me the four macaws, those great gaudy parrots who had been there since the beginning. Rita Hayworth had written in the guest book, "love those crazy parrots—especially Truman!"

The red macaw, Truman Capote, was quite a bird. He greeted the men with, "How are you, Fairy Queen?" To the women he said, "What a pretty pussy," and he usually added, "Aren't you looking older?"

The other three weren't as vocal, though Moctezuma used to shrill "pieces of tail!" instead of "pieces of eight," as was expected of a proper piratical parrot.

They all had earned and deserved a better life, and since Mary and I were headed off for Spain, we couldn't keep them with us. What to do with these talented avian friends? I remembered a fine little zoo in Santa Barbara and wrote to ask if they would like to have four splendid macaws. I had an immediate answer by telegram.

"We accept your generous offer, of course, and await the birds' arrival eagerly. Please inform immediately their previous habitat so that we might duplicate exactly."

I was tempted to answer: "Put the birds in a soft-lit smoky room and keep them up till 2:00 A.M. every night with a background of alcohol-slurred voices, a thumping bass, and a stride piano. Let them hear lots of boozy small talk sprinkled with some genuine esoteric conversation, quite a few dialogues of seduction, marital discords, happy celebrations, the many varied vagaries of the human condition, and so forth. Helpful if you could get Rita Hayworth, Bill Saroyan, and Noel Coward to visit occasionally."

But instead I wired: "Bringing birds down to you Monday and will explain their previous environment. If I can."

For the record, the Matador is still there. Sort of. The bullfighting motif and artifacts disappeared. The big mural I worked so hard on has been covered up with puce material, there are pool tables, and there is no trace of *la fiesta brava* around the electronic pinball machines. Decorators' shops line the Barbary Coast, and Lenny Bruce's ghost cackles around where the Hungry i used to be. From time to time at places like Moose's, I see my longtime bass player, Vernon Alley, who is now a respected member of the prestigious Bohemian Club and former arts commissioner. We get together to reminisce about that golden time and the golden folk in that golden city of yesteryear. And maybe it *was* as good as we think it was. As novelist L. B. Hartley wrote, "The past is a foreign country; they do things differently there."

Or as a character on "The Mary Tyler Moore Show" said, "I didn't like nostalgia then and I don't like it now."

One evening in February, 1994, I drove by the Matador and saw that the sign was down. I peered through a window, and though it was dark, I could see that the place was gutted, piles of lumber indicating that an extensive remodeling job was in progress. Nothing about the place indicated that there had ever been a place called El Matador.

Except! Except the beautiful six-foot mat across the double-door entrance, which announced to the world in black with big white letters, "El Matador." It was the only tangible proof left that there had ever been a place of that name, but it was firmly cemented to the sidewalk. My resolve was instant: Dammit, the Mat's mat mattered! That was my mat, and I must have it forever.

I stationed my wife at the corner to keep an eye out for the fuzz—it would be terribly embarrassing to go to the slammer for vandalism at my time of life. Then I pressed my son, Barny, who was born about the same time as the nightclub, into vigorous action. With one eye cocked for policemen or the new owner, we pulled, yanked, and pried. After ten minutes, the great mat was ripped away from its bed and, like a giant manta ray, was flopped into the trunk of the car. Feeling as though we'd pulled off a monstrous college prank, we drove away jubilantly.

"Just think," I panted. "That mat was trod upon by Ingrid Bergman, Ava Gardner, Rita Hayworth, Marilyn Monroe, Hedy Lamarr, and Vivien Leigh. Plus three Gabors and their mother."

My more literate son added, "And Caldwell, Steinbeck, Capote, and Kerouac."

"Well, it was fun while it lasted," I said.

"I hate that expression," said Mary, "the fun's not over 'till it's over. There's plenty of fun left."

And so now, beautifully scrubbed, the objet d'art glistens in front of the door of our beach house in Santa Barbara, reminding me daily of the illustrious personalities who once crossed the threshold of a Barbary Coast saloon in the great city of San Francisco so long ago, and of a way of life lamentably long gone that lives only in a few people's memories and in the musty pages of a leatherbound guest book in my living room.